GETTING
HIGH
NATURALLY

Books in the YOUTH WORLD Series

Popular Song & Youth Today

Contemporary Film & the *New* Generation

Peace, War & Youth

Love & Hate

Touch With Love

Getting High Naturally

GETTING HIGH NATURALLY

Edited by
LOUIS M. SAVARY

ASSOCIATION PRESS
New York, N.Y.

GETTING HIGH NATURALLY
Copyright © 1971 by Association Press
291 Broadway, New York, N.Y. 10007

All rights reserved. No part of this publication may be reprinted, reproduced, transmitted, stored in a retrieval system, or otherwise utilized, in any form or by any means, electronic or mechanical, including photocopying or recording, now existing or hereinafter invented, without the prior written permission of the publisher.

Standard Book Number: 8096-1819-2
Library of Congress Catalog Card Number: 74-152898
Printed in the United States of America

ACKNOWLEDGMENTS

Many of the works from which selections herein are taken are protected by copyright, and may not be reproduced in any form without the consent of the authors, their publishers, or their agents. Every effort has been made to trace the ownership of all selections in this book and to obtain the necessary authorization for their use. If any errors or omissions have occurred in this regard, corrections will be made in all future editions of this book. Since the copyright page cannot legibly accommodate all the acknowledgments and copyright notices, this page and the pages following constitute an extension of the copyright page.

Grateful acknowledgment is made to:
Conrad Aiken for permission to reprint a selection from his poem "Evensong"; *California Law Review* for selection by Alan W. Watts from "Psychedelics and Religious Experience," 1968; Challenge Press, Inc. for selection by Robert H. Rimmer from *The Rebellion of Yale Marratt*, 1964; Collier Books for selections by Bernard Gunther from *Sense Relaxation Below Your Mind*, 1968; Delacorte Press for selections by George B. Leonard from *Education and Ecstasy*. Copyright © 1968 by George B. Leonard. Used by permission; Doubleday & Company, Inc. for selection by Margaret Mead from *Culture and Commitment: A Study of the Generation Gap*, 1970, for Navaho Indian and Passamaquoddy Indian songs from *Technicians of the Sacred*, ed. by Jerome Rothberg, 1968, for selection by Ira Einhorn from "From Data Collection to Pattern Recognition: the Sociology of the Now," in *Psychedelics*, ed. Bernard Aaronson and Humphry Osmond, 1970, and for selection by John W. Aiken from "The Church of the Awakening"; Emile Durckheim for selection from *The Japanese Cult of Tranquility*, 1960; Ira Einhorn for selection from "Change, Media, Communication," 1970; Professor Angel Flores for permission to reprint Edward Mörike's "The Wind's Song"; Grove Press, Inc. for selections by William C. Schutz from *Joy: Expanding Human Awareness*, 1967; Harcourt, Brace & Jovanovich, Inc. for selection by Mircea Eliade from *The Sacred and the Profane*, 1959; *Ingenue* for selection by Laurie Muir; Ione Hill for permission to reprint poems from *Three-Eyed Pieces*, 1967; *Hit Parader* for selection by Keith Richards, 1971, and for interview with

Melanie Safka; McGraw-Hill Book Company for selections by André Breton and Thorbecke, reprinted in Suzanne Lilar's *Aspects of Love*, 1965, and for selection by Jane Howard from *Please Touch*, 1970; Albin Michel, Paris, for selection by Jean-Jacques Trillat from *Exploring the Structure of Matter*, 1956; The New American Library for selection by Alfred North Whitehead from *Science and the Modern World*, 1933; *New York Times Magazine* for selection by Joseph Adelson; New York University Press for selection by E. S. Morgan from *Visible Saints*, 1963; *Newsweek* for selection by Walter Lippmann; Pantheon Books, Inc. for selections by Alan W. Watts from *Nature, Man, and Woman*, 1958; Paulist-Newman Press for selection by Karl Rahner from *Encounters With Silence*, 1960; Random House, Inc. for selection by Jonathan Eisen from *The Age of Rock*, 1969, for selection by Norman O. Brown from *Love's Body*, 1966, and for selection by Alan W. Watts from *The Joyous Cosmology*, 1962; Henry Regnery Co. for selection by Jean Daniélou from *Lord of History*, 1958; *Rolling Stone* for selection by Ralph J. Gleason, 1970; Alice Sullivan for permission to reprint her poem.

Photo Credits: Karen Becker 59, 62, 84-85, 103; Leslie Becker 65, 73; Ettie de Láczay 104, 156-157; Valentine Echo 45, 101; Maury Englander 106-107, 126-127; Joseph Ferrara 75; Laurence Fink, 23, 25; Finnish National Travel Office 66, 128; Mimi Forsyth 152; German Information Center 43; Israeli Tourist Office 113; Japan 96-97; Seymour Linden 46, 57, 90-91, 158; Fortune Monte 79, 109, 142, 144, 149; Jacques-Clarence Paucker 123; Sylvia Plachy 10, 34-35, 37, 50-51, 83, 95, 117, 125, 141, 151, 154; Abe Rezny 41, 98, 133, 146; Shelly Rusten 15, 17, 20, 26, 29, 30, 69, 121, 136, 138-139; David Sagarin 18, 71, 88-89, 119, 130; Paul Shapiro 13, 32, 54; Swedish National Tourist Office 39, 49, 53, 61, 76, 80-81, 86, 92, 110-111; Swiss National Tourist Office 114; Wayne Wiebel 135.

CONTENTS

Acknowledgments 5
Preface 9
Living a Death 11
Living Can Be More Than This 21
The Way of Drugs 27
Getting There Without Drugs 33
Sensory Awakening 38
A New Way of Seeing 47
A Magical World All My Own 55
Even in the Everyday World 63
The Way of Music 68
The Gypsy Spirit 74
Experiencing Things 82
The Universe is Alive and Ready 91
My Body in the Universe 99
My Self, Unique and Alone 106
I Am More Than Mind 112
Transformation 118
Joy and Creative Imagination 124
Freedom and the Future 131
Others and All Others 136
Facing Love 143
Together From Eternity 148
Love Unifying the Boundless 154

PREFACE

Young people today are searching for a way to turn on to life. They look anxiously in many directions for clues to vital and full human experiences. Few are able to find a way. Many try drugs and are enthusiastic about their mind-expanding experiences. But in the end they are threatened by drug laws, or victimized by deadly stuff (for example, it is reliably reported that there is no clean LSD on the market today), or they are caught by the psychedelic spider in his choking web of drug addiction. Often those young people most eager for life are destroyed.

But there are other ways of getting high — quiet, unsuspected, often unobtrusive ways. A few very special people throughout the centuries have discovered drugless pathways in the uncharted caverns of the mind. Many courageous pioneers exploring new creative states of consciousness, today have entered the dimensions of peace, love and unity throbbing at the heart of each living thing. They seek to know and feel what very few other humans have ever known or experienced.

Getting High Naturally presents people who have achieved the high experience without chemical catalysts. In their writings they share with us the bits and pieces of insight they have gathered into the life vision that lies in store for those who follow them.

LIVING A DEATH

"Most men lead lives of quiet desperation," wrote Thoreau almost a century ago. And the statement is still true today. Use whatever word you prefer—boredom, frustration, ennui, anomie, meaninglessness. Most people find life dull. And that's a sad situation. For the whole point of life is to be fully aware of it as it happens, to find living exciting, mysterious, entrancing.

Few people really learn to relax in the sounds and sights of life, enjoy the feel of things, and luxuriate in the full experience of what it means to be alive. Listening to the vibrations of what's happening might distract the successful executive from business, or cause a loss in sales, or harm savings accounts, or slow down paper work. People make plans to retire—to begin life at sixty-five. People are eager to live, and so very few know how. It is not going to happen magically at sixty-five. Now is the time, while young, to learn how to escape from the boredom of life.

But dropouts and graduates alike
have had plenty of practice
in fragmenting their lives—
segregating senses from emotions from intellect,
building boxes for art and abstractions,
divorcing the self from the reality
and the joy of the present moment.

               George B. Leonard

The whole point of life
is to be fully aware of it as it happens.
One therefore relaxes, almost luxuriously,
into studying the colors in a glass of water,
or in listening to the now
highly articulate vibration
of every note played on an oboe
or sung by a voice.

From the pragmatic standpoint of our culture,
such an attitude is very bad for business.
It might lead to improvidence,
lack of foresight,
diminished sales of insurance policies,
and abandoned savings accounts.
Yet this is just the corrective
that our culture needs.

No one is more fatuously impractical
than the "successful" executive
who spends his whole life
absorbed in frantic paper work
with the objective
of retiring in comfort at sixty-five,
when it will all be too late.

Only those who have cultivated
the art of living completely in the present
have any use for making plans
for the future,
for when the plans mature
they will be able to enjoy the results.

Alan Watts

The young generation,
the articulate young rebels
all around the world
who are lashing out against the controls
to which they are subjected,
are like the first generation
born into a new country.

They are at home in this time.
Satellites are familiar in their skies.
They have never known a time
when war did not threaten annihilation.
Those who use computers do not
         anthropomorphize them...

They live in a world in which
events are presented to them
in all their complex immediacy;
they are no longer bound
by the simplified linear sequences
dictated by the printed word.

In their eyes the killing of an enemy
is not qualitatively different
from the murder of a neighbor.

                    Margaret Mead

In these images,
and in our tendency
to identify ourselves with them,
we can discover
the alienation within all of us,
old and young.
We use the young to represent
our despair,
our violence,
our often forlorn hopes
for a better world.

       Joseph Adelson

LIVING CAN BE MORE THAN THIS

If there is one fact true of a living person it is this: if he hasn't achieved his full human potential, he isn't living as fully as possible.

Think of the hidden talents, undeveloped skills, untapped abilities—all the potential for excellence, enjoyment, creativity. The human potential is probably our largest untapped human resource. The capacity for achieving the natural high is a part of this untapped potential. In releasing and refining the special energies many have discovered exhilaration that equals or surpasses the chemical high.

We regard evolution as primarily
transformation of mind...
the story of life is
no more than a movement of consciousness
veiled by changes in biological structure...
as children of a transition period,
we are neither fully conscious of,
nor in full control of,
the new powers that have been unleashed.

                Pierre Teilhard de Chardin

The rate of present cultural change,
though fast becoming visible,
far exceeds the ability
and tools of the experts
who are attempting to measure it;
it is not a measurable quantity.

What is happening
cannot be easily delimited
by the man with perspective
who stands without.
Only those who are involved
have a faint chance of being able
to describe the ongoing as it goes on.
We can't depend on the past,
for that which is now has never been before.

    Ira Einhorn

THE WAY OF DRUGS

Some young people have attempted to break out of the boredom and frustration of life by using drugs. From ages ten to thirty all across the nation, people are using drugs to turn on, to get high, but mainly to escape. Unfortunately, at best the effects of drugs are unpredictable. Many drug experiences turn out to be bitter, destructive, some disastrous. The number of hard-drug addicts grows each day—burdening the human family with an uncreative sickness.

I'm twenty-six now and I've been on drugs since I was fifteen. My father was a diplomat in Calcutta then, and I happened to come by some opium. I took it, and, well, it's always the same story after that, and I won't bore you with it. I used to write poetry then, and paint. It probably wasn't very good, but after I got hooked I stopped doing anything at all. I married, but my habit ruined that as well. My wife left me.... I don't blame her. Last year, I was in Europe. I took an overdose by mistake, and nearly died. Then a little later I couldn't get any at all, and that nearly killed me too. You've no idea of the pain when you can't get it—physical and mental. Imagine the worst pain you can think of, multiply it ten thousand times, and you'll still have no idea.

John

The spectacle of drug abuse astonishes those physicians and pharmacologists who are well aware of the hazards of these agents. In some instances the potential dangers are hardly known at this time. The reward-danger ratio is too high a price to pay. It seems inevitable that the misuse will recede eventually, but not before many valuable people have been psychologically, physically or socially impaired.

Sidney Cohen

I swear, gentlemen,
that to be too conscious
is an illness,
a real, thoroughgoing illness.

Fyodor Dostoevsky

> Just as madness is the beginning of all wisdom,
> so is schizomania the beginning of all art
> > and fantasy.
>
> > > Herman Hesse

I laid off five years ago,
and if anyone asks my advice today,
I tell him to steer clear of it
because it carries a rap.
That's my final word to all you cats:
today I know of one very bad thing
the tea can do—
it can put you in jail.

> Mezz Mezzrow

GETTING THERE WITHOUT DRUGS

Psychedelic drugs have enabled people to make quick journeys into unexplored lands of the mind and have opened up new avenues of the possible. But psychologists testify that many people have been able to experience over and over again a natural high... without drugs. In this way the "psychic mobility rudely thrust upon one by the psychedelics can be learned with no drugs whatsoever." Natural paths to a fuller experience are open to everyone, ways that people have always known existed. We are moving into the age of the natural high.

The psychedelics have provided
quick journeys into other lands of the mind;
they have expanded
many people's concept of the possible.
Even here, however,
it is becoming clear
that the kind of psychic mobility
rudely thrust upon one by the psychedelics
can be learned with no drugs whatever.

                    George B. Leonard

It's an experience that we have
at some stage to go through...
Things have got to impinge upon us
until we gradually build ourselves up
into an acceptance of reality,
and a greater and greater
acceptance of reality
and what really exists—
and any dodging of it only delays the time
and it's just as if you were
going to sea in a boat
that was not really capable
of dealing with the storms that can rise.

Jesse Watkins

The current interest in LSD and other psychedelic drugs has a relation to the joy techniques. The aims are similar—to make the experience of life more vital. The joy methods attempt to achieve this without drugs. How similar the experiences are I don't know personally, but several people who have experienced both feel there are some close similarities.

William C. Schutz

It is desire that builds the mountain
And the way to climb it.
It is desire that life lives.

              Ione Hill

SENSORY AWAKENING

Enjoyment of life is always free. It comes of its own accord, spontaneously. One cannot force happiness or squeeze pleasure out of an experience. It simply happens. Happiness is not an object-out-there, something to be bought or grasped in one's hands. It is rather a way of being, the person himself filled from within with an aliveness which we call happiness. "Awakening" is a metaphor to express the change of consciousness in a person who passes from a state of boredom, like sleep, to an experience of being turned on to life.

Everything should be dancing,
every particle of life
should pulsate with joy.
The world is made for the living.
It was constructed to entertain
and sustain humanity.

    David Kohn

You can't know what it's like to be alive
until you've been a thief
in a dark room where someone is sleeping.
There's no way I can tell you—
how *awake* you are,
how much you can hear—
you can hear with your skin—
how much you *know*.
There's a police car moving over there
three blocks away.
You *know* it's there.
You sense it.
You *feel* it moving . . .

            A thief

Sensory Awakening is . . .
A way to allow direct experience,
a return to primary process.
Unfiltered contact
with what is on going
without expectation
or excessive inhibition.
No sense of separation;
meditation, being in the now.
Oneness in this happening moment.

           Bernard Gunther

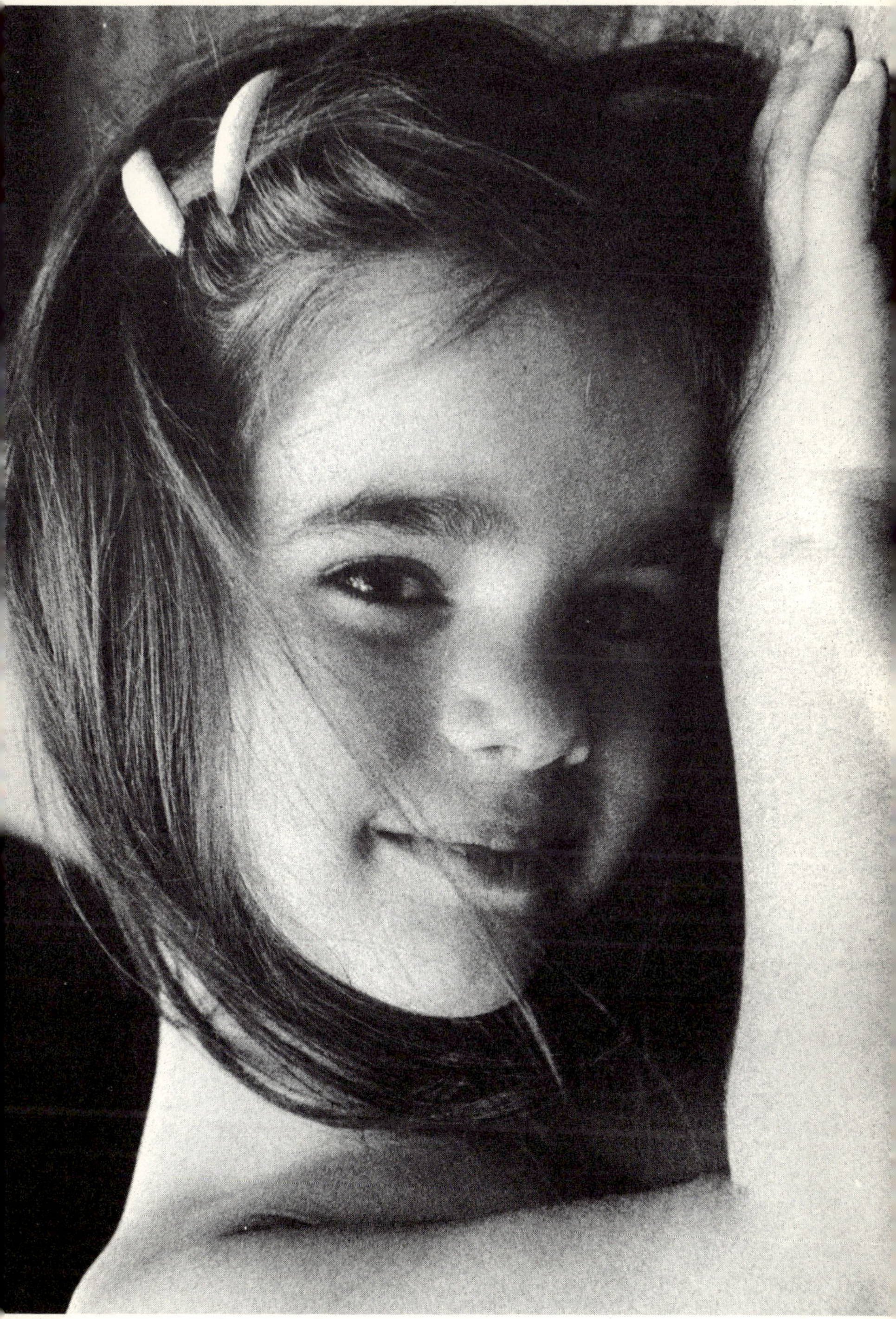

Enjoyment is always gratuitous
and can come no other way
than of itself, spontaneously.
To try to force it is, furthermore,
to try to experience the future
before it has arrived,
to seek the psychological *result*
of attending to the present experience
and thus short-circuiting
or cutting out the experience itself.

Obviously, however, the person
who attempts to get something
from his present experience
feels divided from it.
He is the subject
and it is the object.

He does not see
that he *is* that experience,
and that trying to get something from it
is merely self-pursuit.

    Alan Watts

People who "peak" can transcend the mundane
and feel ecstatically fulfilled.
The stimulus for that ecstasy
is as hard to guess
as next week's weather,
but its quality
is unmistakable.

     Jane Howard

O World invisible, we view thee,
O World intangible, we touch thee,
O World unknowable, we know thee,
Inapprehensible, we clutch thee!

Does the fish soar to find the ocean,
The eagle plunge to find the air—
That we ask of the stars in motion
If they have rumour of thee there?

Not where the wheeling systems darken,
And our benumbed conceiving soars!—
The drift of pinions, would we hearken,
Beats at our own clay-shuttered doors.

The angels keep their ancient places;—
Turn but a stone, and start a wing!
'Tis ye, 'tis your estranged faces,
That miss the many-splendoured thing.

     Francis Thompson

Does the Eagle know what is in the pit,
Or wilt thou go ask the Mole?
Can Wisdom be put in a silver rod?
Or Love in a golden bowl?

     William Blake

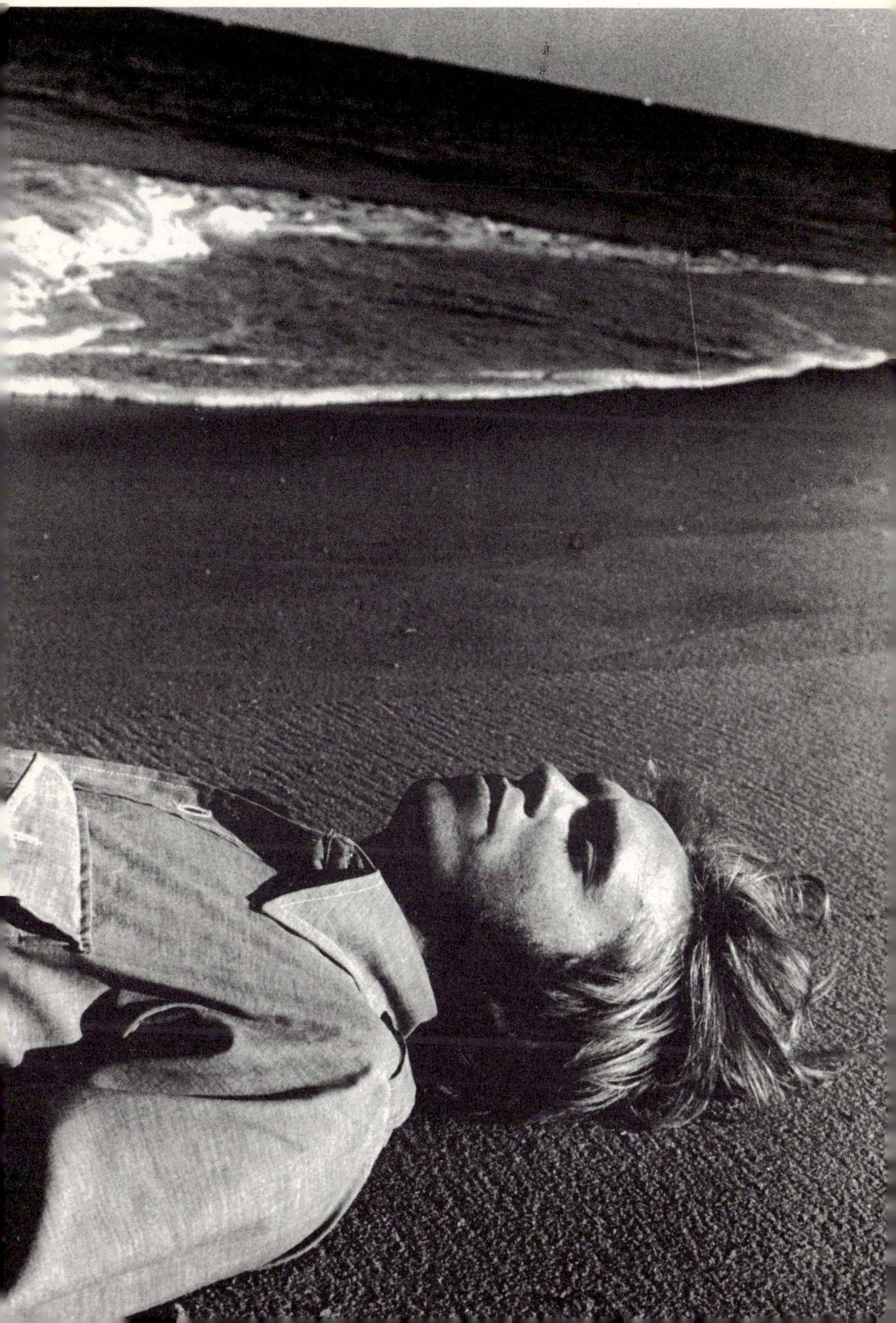

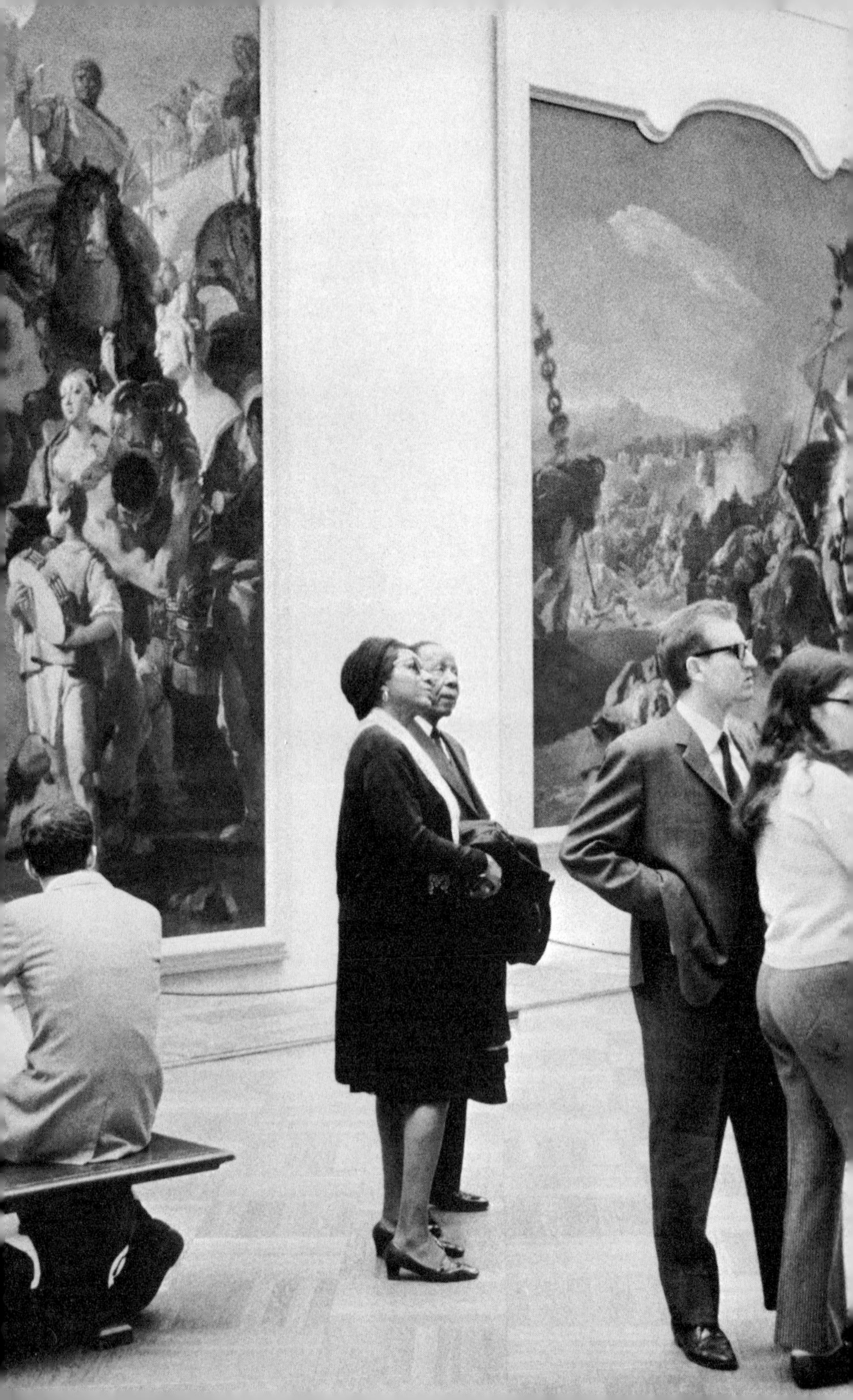

A NEW WAY OF SEEING

Children know the experience of ecstasy, but they learn to unlearn it as they grow older. There is no need to abdicate this experience. Life can remain full of intense insight, full of visions into things around us that transform our world into something splendid and wonderful. Some would call this a new way of seeing, or seeing beyond seeing. Others would describe the experience as carrying the whole world within you.

As long as the symbol of the tree
does not awaken his total consciousness
and "open" it to the universe,
it cannot be said to have
completely fulfilled its function.
It has only partly "saved" him
from his individual situation—
for example, by enabling him
to resolve a deep crisis
and restoring his temporarily threatened
psychic equilibrium;
but it has not yet raised him to spirituality—
that is, it has not succeeded in revealing
one of the structures of the real to him.

       Mircea Eliade

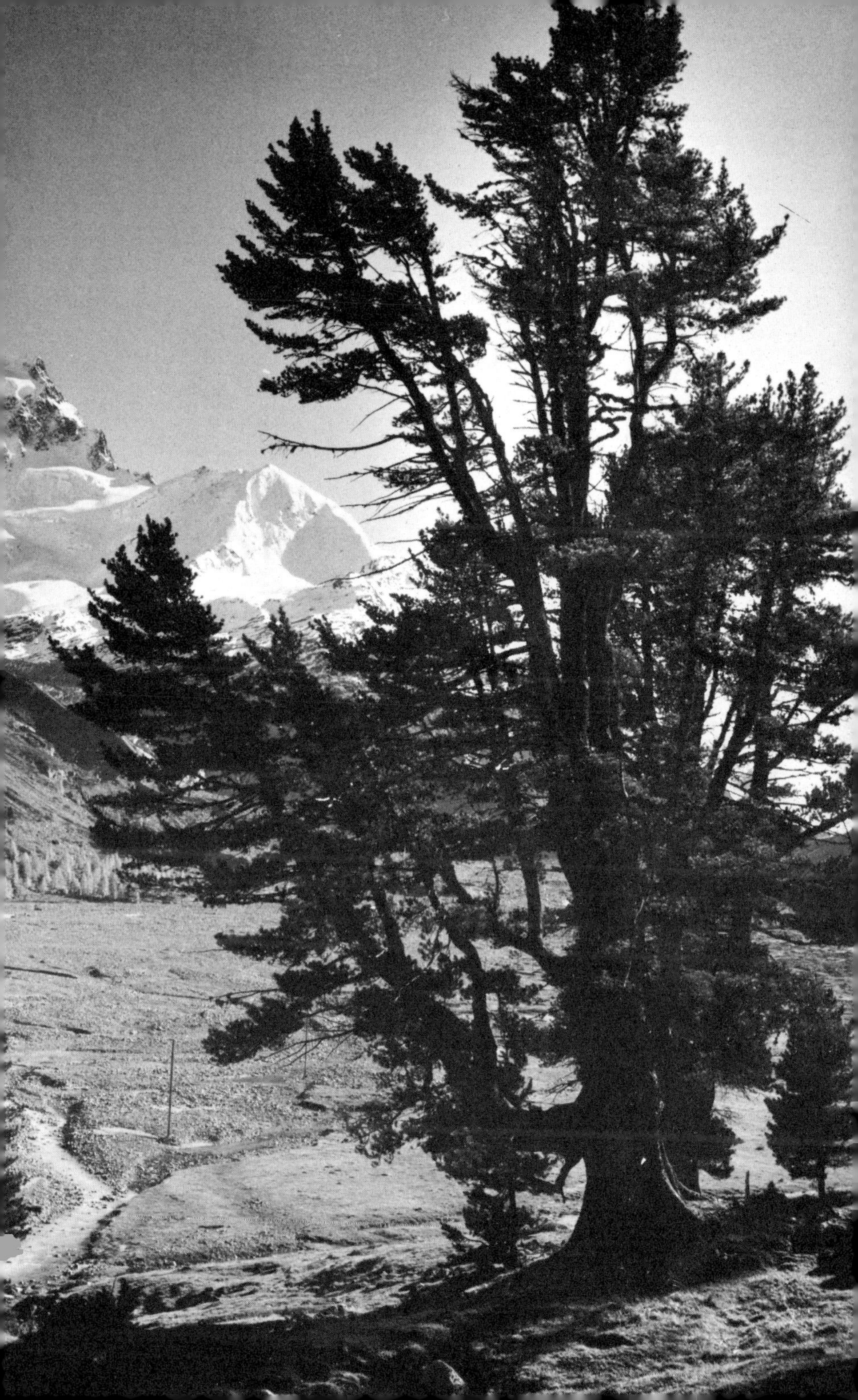

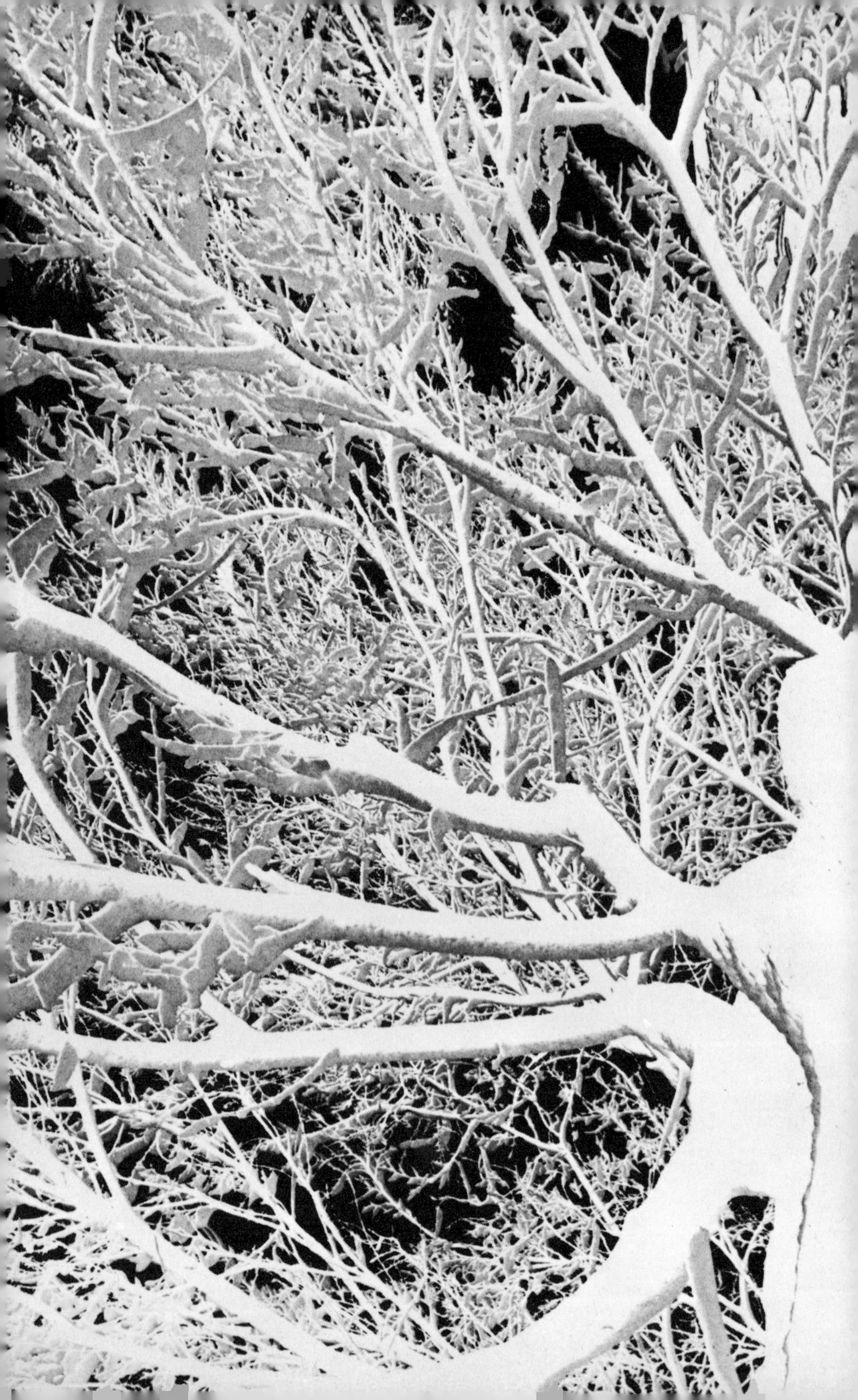

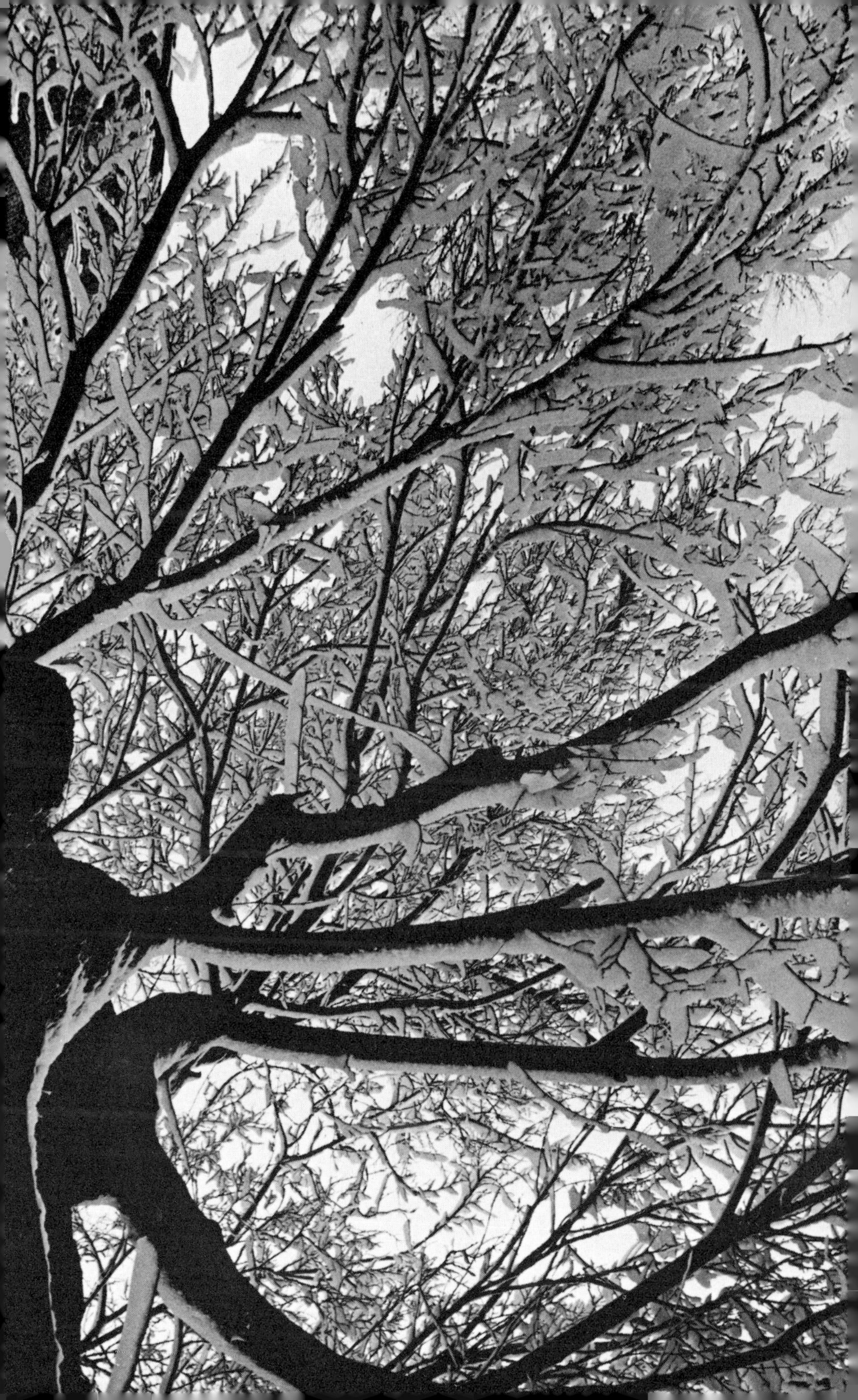

In beauty I walk
With beauty before me I walk
With beauty behind me I walk
With beauty above me I walk
With beauty above and about me I walk
It is finished in beauty
It is finished in beauty.

    Navaho Indian night chant

The world
is God's
language
to us.
Simone Weil

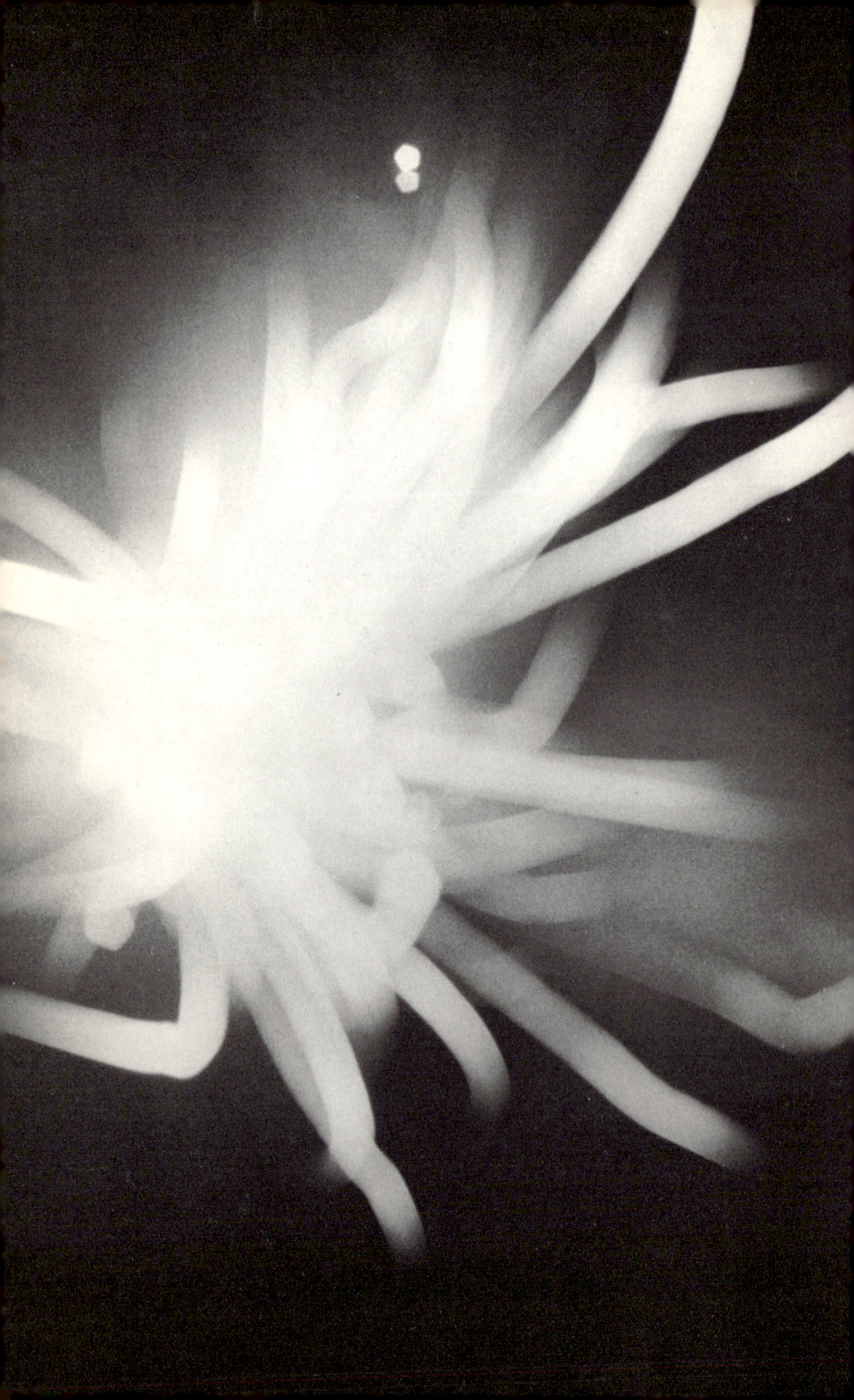

A MAGICAL WORLD ALL MY OWN

In experiencing a high, a person feels at one with everything. "The organism and its surrounding world," writes Alan Watts, "are a single, integrated pattern of action." The person takes upon himself a kind of superconsciousness that dissolves all divisions between the self and nature. He is not merely in nature but of it. As if by magic, he and everything around him are transformed into a new living thing.

Summer is a sailor in a rowboat
and ice cream on your dress
when you're four years old.
Summer is a man with his coat off,
wet sand between your toes,
the smell of a garden
an hour before moonrise.
Oh, summer is silk itself,
a giant geranium
and music from a flute far away.

        Michael Brown

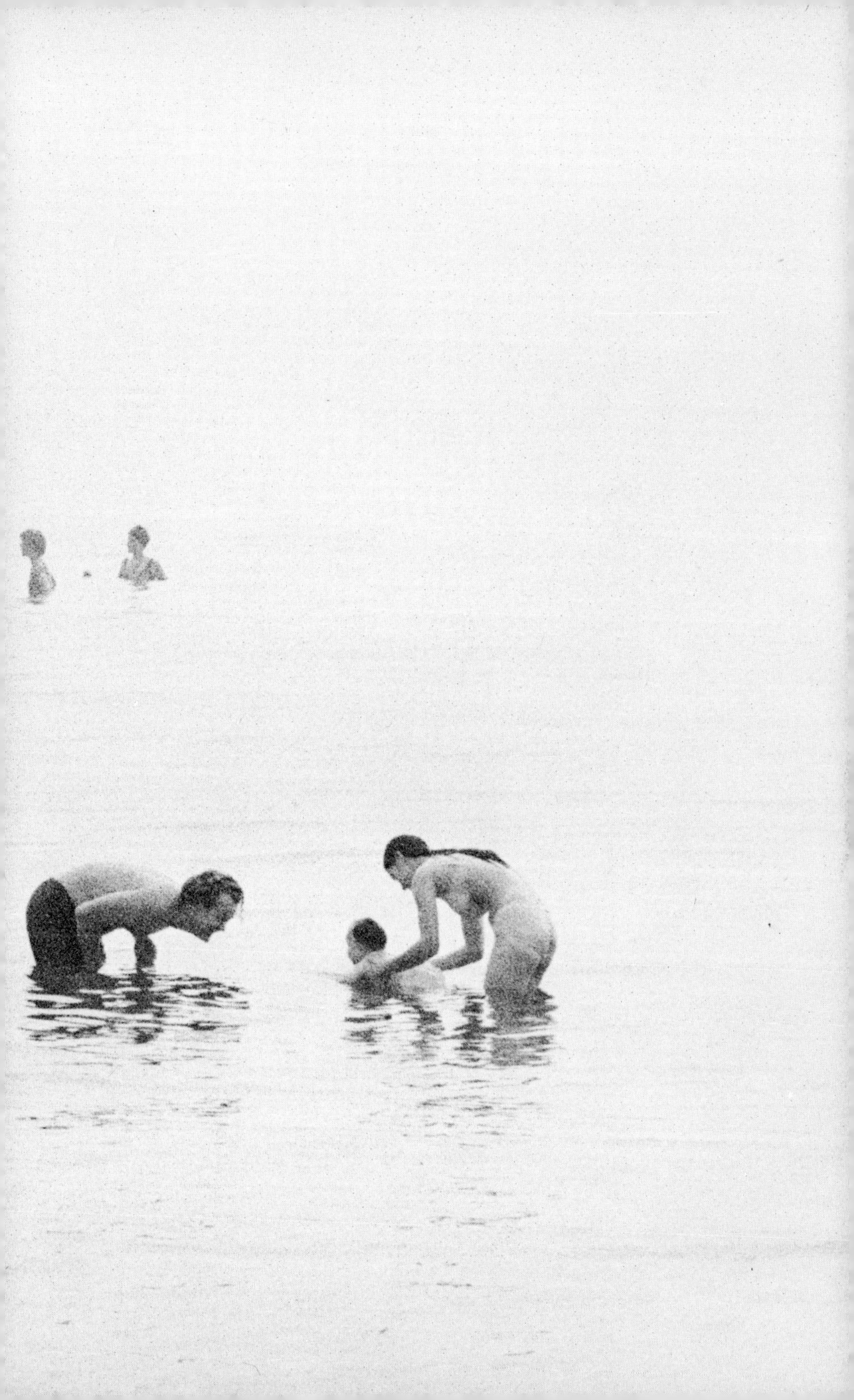

This world,
after all our science and sciences,
is still a miracle;
wonderful, inscrutable,
magical and more,
to whosoever will think of it.

        Thomas Carlyle

For we are the stars. For we sing.
For we sing with our light.
For we are birds made of fire.
For we spread our wings over the sky.
Our light is a voice.
We cut a road for the soul
for its journey through death.

        Passamaquoddy Indian song

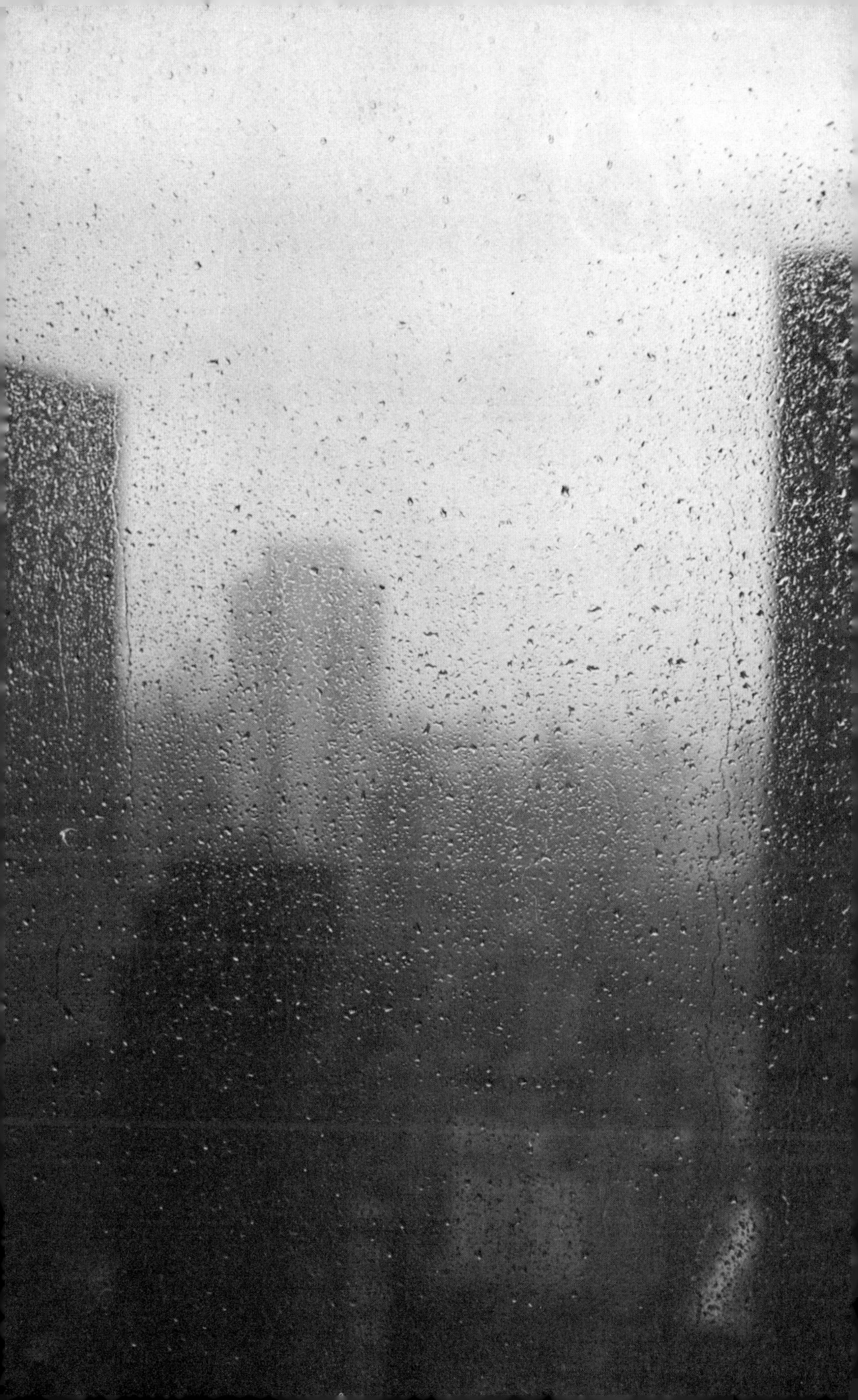

When you understand all about the sun
and all about the atmosphere
and all about the rotation of the earth,
you may still miss
the radiance of the sunset.
There is no substitute
for the direct perception (*kuan*)
of the concrete achievement
of a thing in its actuality.

        Alfred North Whitehead

Among all the strange things
that men have forgotten,
the most universal lapse of memory
is that they are living on a star.

        G. K. Chesterton

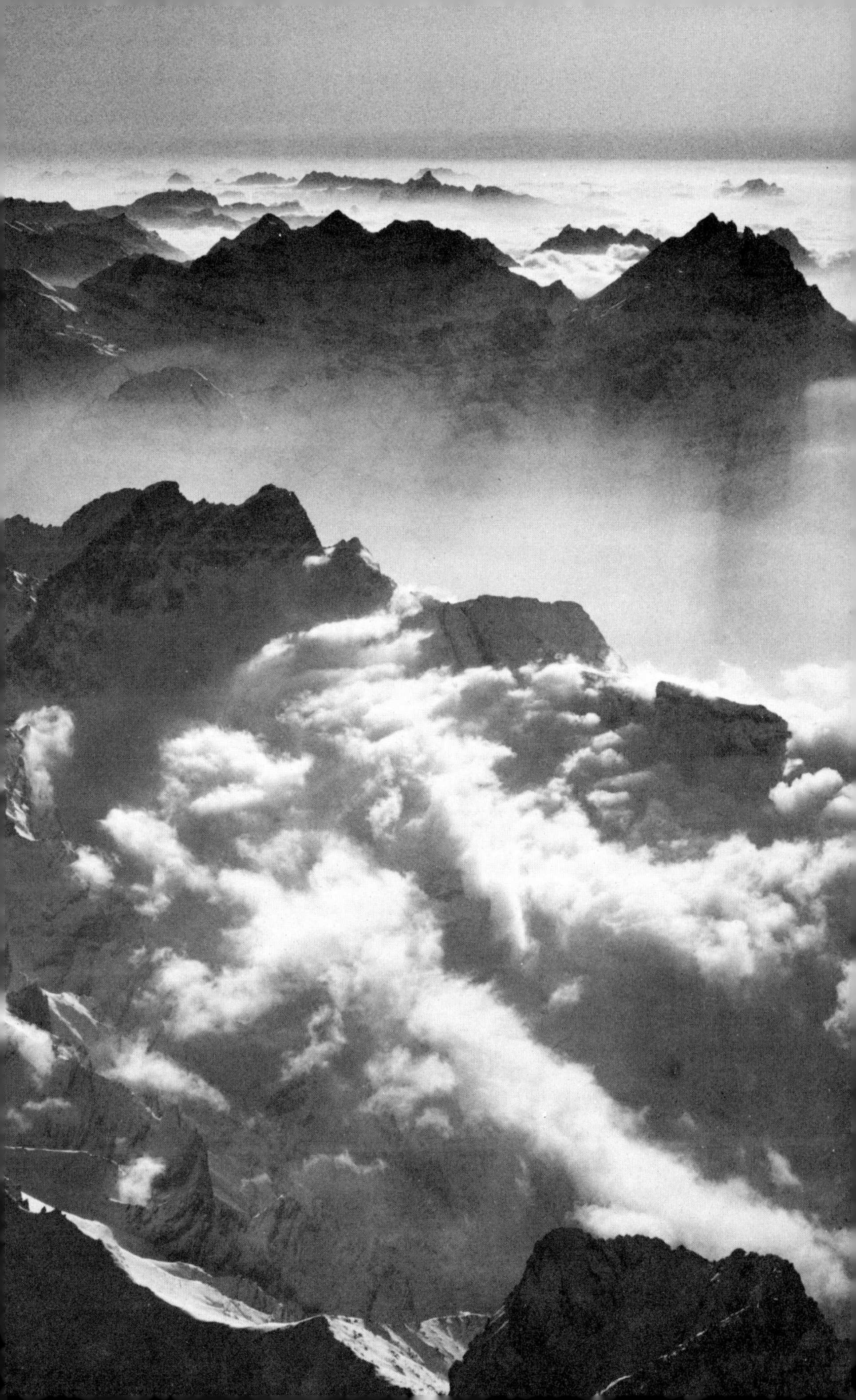

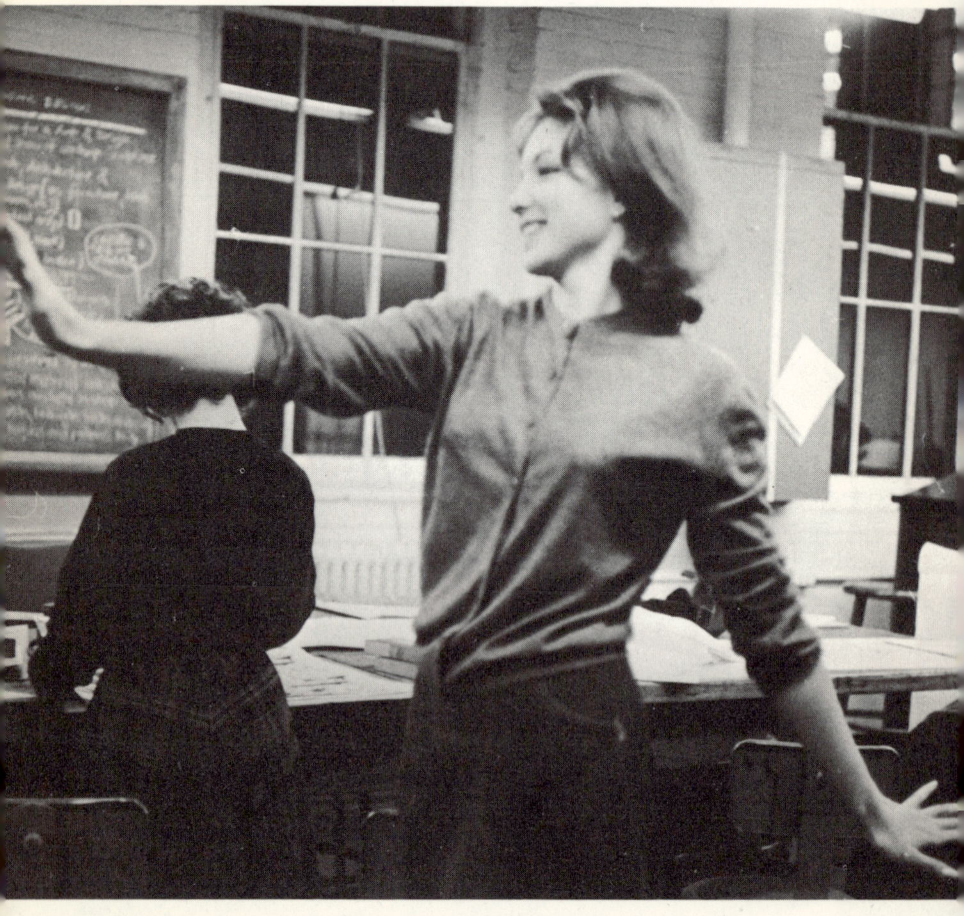

EVEN IN THE EVERYDAY WORLD

The high experience is not limited to mountains and sunsets. It can happen even in the everyday world of pots and pans and papers and pencils, as long as such experiences are greeted with openness and awareness. When a person learns to get high on the most common experiences of a busy day, he can become a new kind of human being.

The next time you do dishes,
be sensitive to shapes,
temperatures, textures,
bursting soap bubbles.
Get rid of your expectations—
it's going to be a drag;
I'm not going to enjoy this—
and allow yourself to be
wholly aware.

        Bernard Gunther

Converting the feeling
into a total body-experience
makes it much more meaningful.

        William C. Schutz

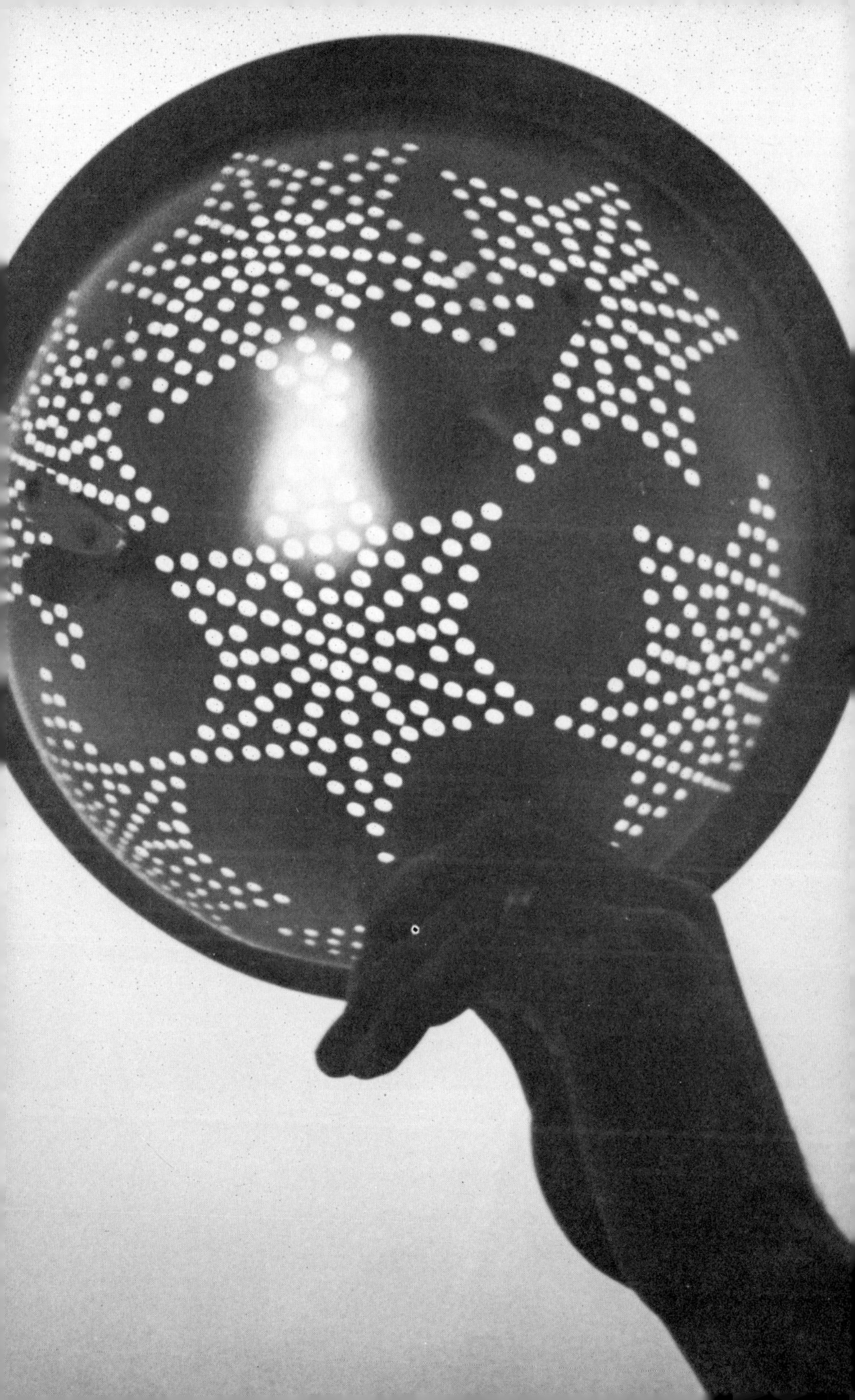

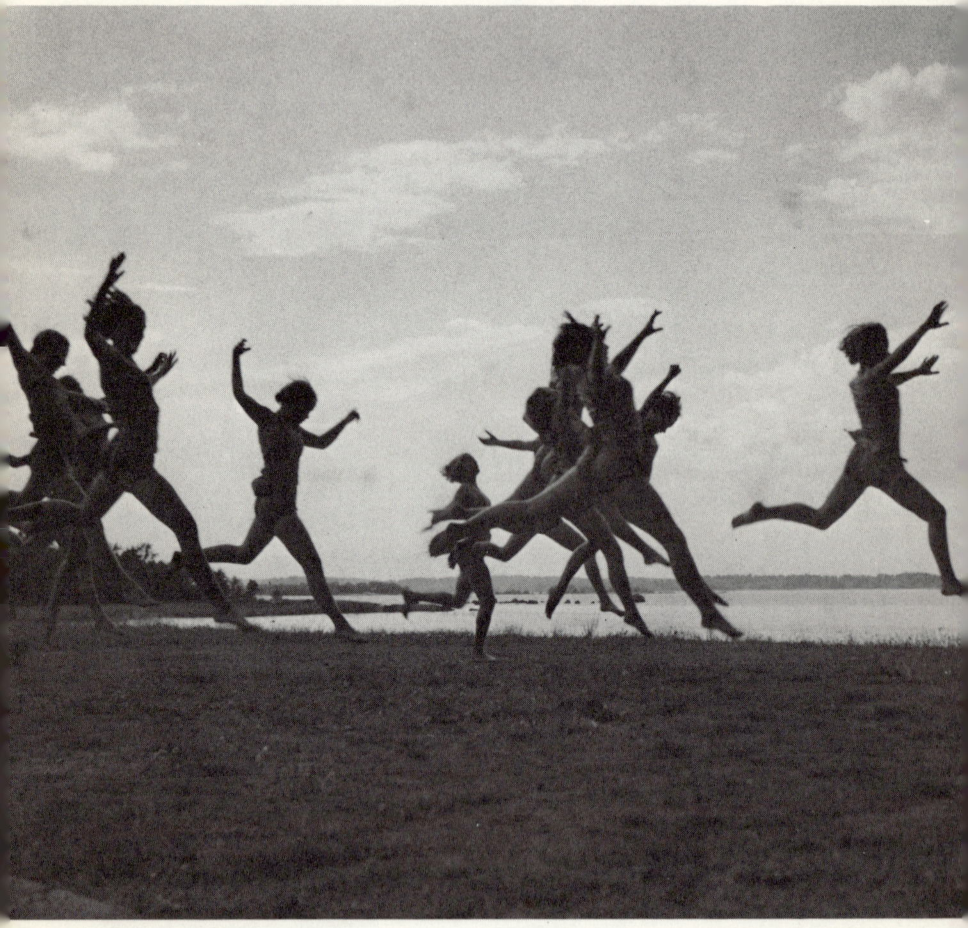

You must always be drunk. It is the only duty. Not to feel the horrible burden of time breaking your shoulders and bowing you towards the ground, you must get drunk without stopping.

But on what? Not on wine, but on sky, on poetry, on waterskiing, on virtue, on the Bible, on love—after your fashion. But get drunk!

And sometimes it will happen that—on the stadium ramp, in the green grass of a ditch, in the dreary solitude of your own room—you will wake up, with your drunkenness already lessened or gone. What to do then? Ask wind, wave, star, bird, clock, everything that flees, murmurs, rolls, sings, speaks: Ask them what time it is. And wind, wave, star, bird, clock will answer you: "It is time to get drunk! Not to be the tormented slaves of Time, get drunk without stopping! On sky, or poetry, or waterskiing, or virtue, or the Bible, or love — after your fashion."

Samuel Willoughby
(<i>after Baudelaire</i>)

THE WAY OF MUSIC

For many young people music and dance will provide a familiar door to the natural high experience. Music has a way of getting through, into our minds, into our feelings and even into our bones—insinuating its way delicately into the brain as with classical European and Oriental music, slamming straight to the viscera as with hard rock, or making melody with the heart as with pop tunes of the '70's.

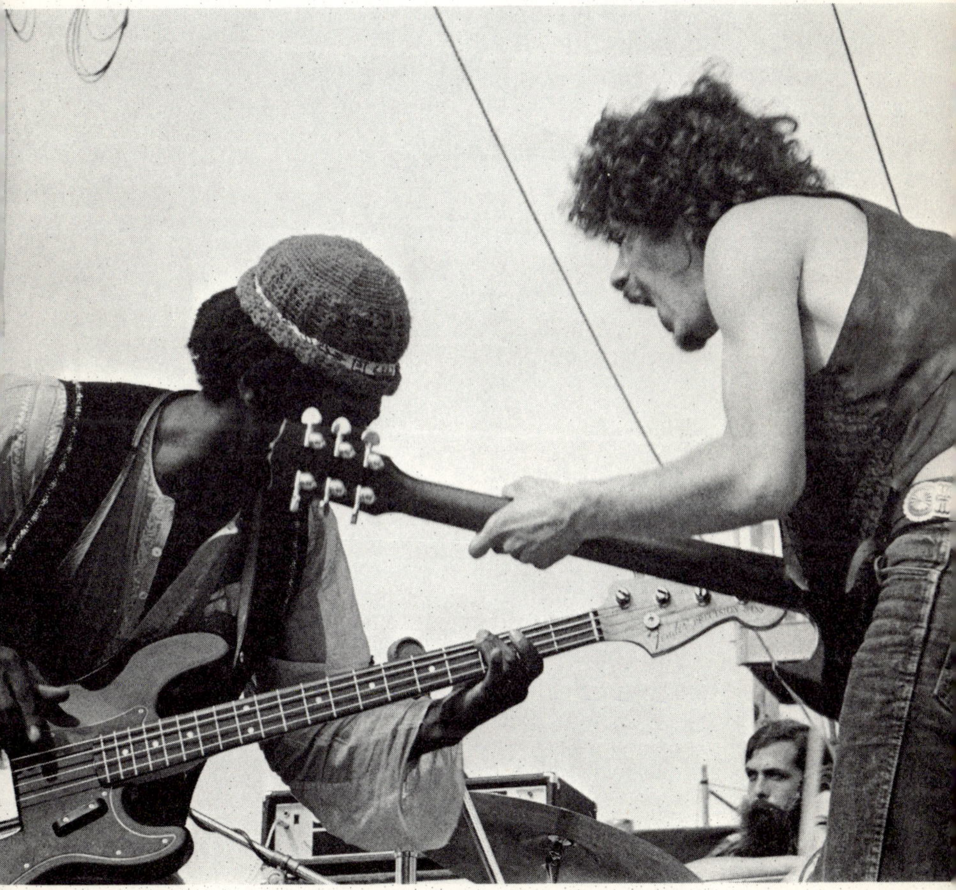

If I've got half an hour,
I just sit down and play.
I don't sit down
with the intention of writing,
it is merely to play the guitar.
After about half an hour
of playing songs I really dig—
old songs by blues people—
I start playing
whatever comes into my head
and I start writing
from the mistakes I make,
because I think,
"Oh, that might sound nice."

      Keith Richards

    Best of all were the moments
    when Stevie Winwood threw back his head
    and let his voice climb
    step by step,
    until you could see
    yet another picture—
    a homesick eagle seeking the sun.

        The New York *Times*

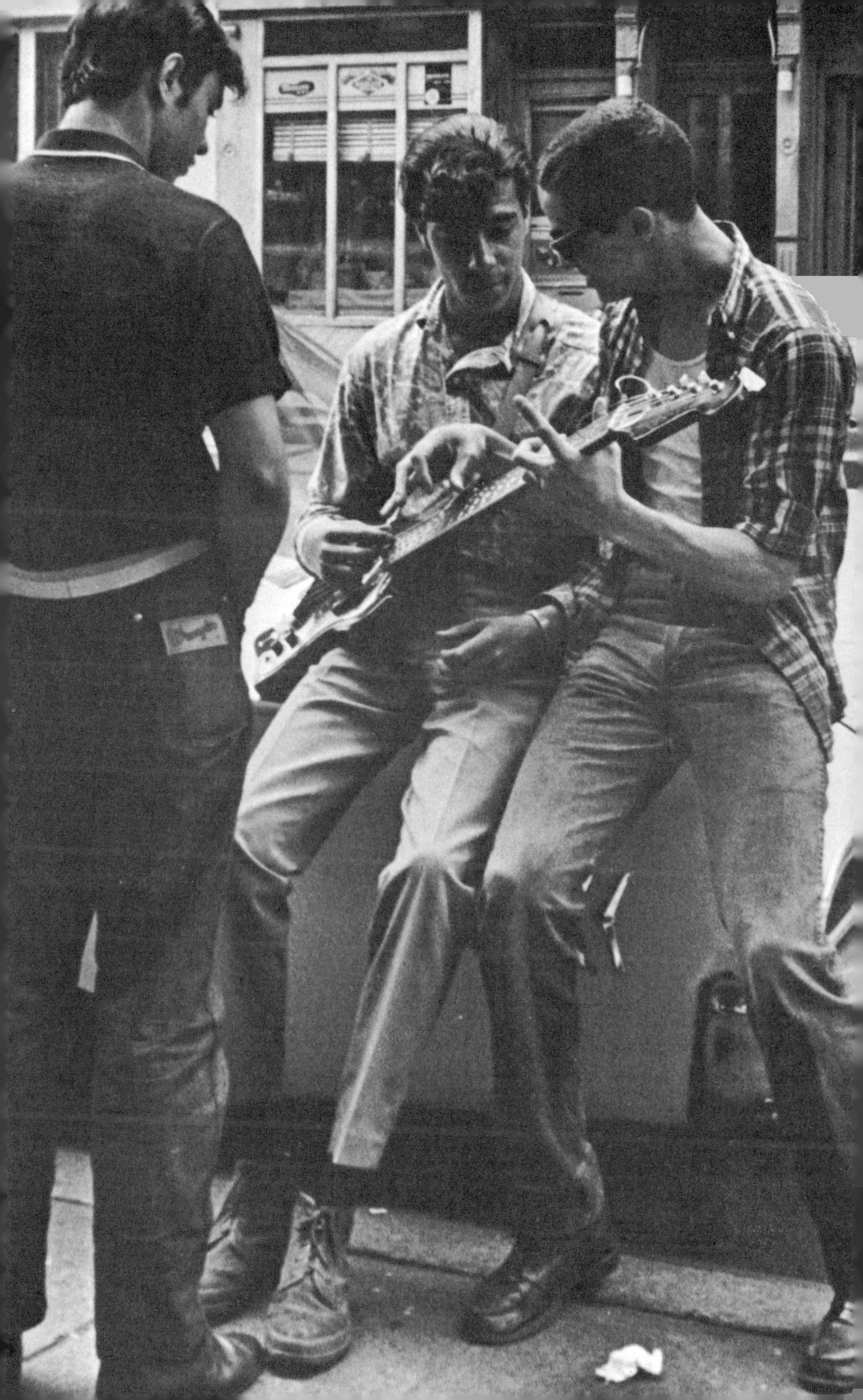

Then Janis stomped her foot
and shook her hair
and started to scream.
They held still
for a couple of seconds,
but here and there
in the great sunlit arena,
longhairs started getting up
and stomping along with the band...
The Monterey County Fairgrounds arena
was packed with people
writhing
and snaking along
in huge chains.
Nothing like it had ever happened before
in the festival's ten years
and nothing like it has happened since.
It was Janis' day,
no doubt about it.
She turned them on
like they had not been turned on in years...
old and young,
long hair and short,
black or white...

        Ralph J. Gleason

        I wonder when it was
        that we merged with our music,
        when we became aware
        that rock was not only our music
        but it was us and we were it,
        that we not only listened to the music,
        grooved and danced
        and loved and tripped to it
        but actually became what it was,

lived many of us a life of music;
that we were defined by it
and realized that it
was an integral part,
possibly the only integral part
of our lives.
When we woke up
one fine morning as I did,
put on Goodday Sunshine
to celebrate the new day
and knew that somehow
I had merged a part of me
with the Beatles
who themselves had become a part of me.

        Jonathan Eisen

THE GYPSY SPIRIT

Everyone has felt the call of the road, the wanderlust that drives one off in search of adventure and excitement. Some feel most alive when they are about to set off somewhere. The world is—and always has been—filled with travelers. How many of them know they are searching for new ways of being alive? How many know that they seek uprooting to end the alienation of the familiar land whose repeated stimuli no longer lift the spirit?

But the true travelers
are only those who depart
for the sake of departing;
with hearts light as balloons,
they never avoid their destiny
and always say: Let us go!
without knowing why.

       Charles Baudelaire

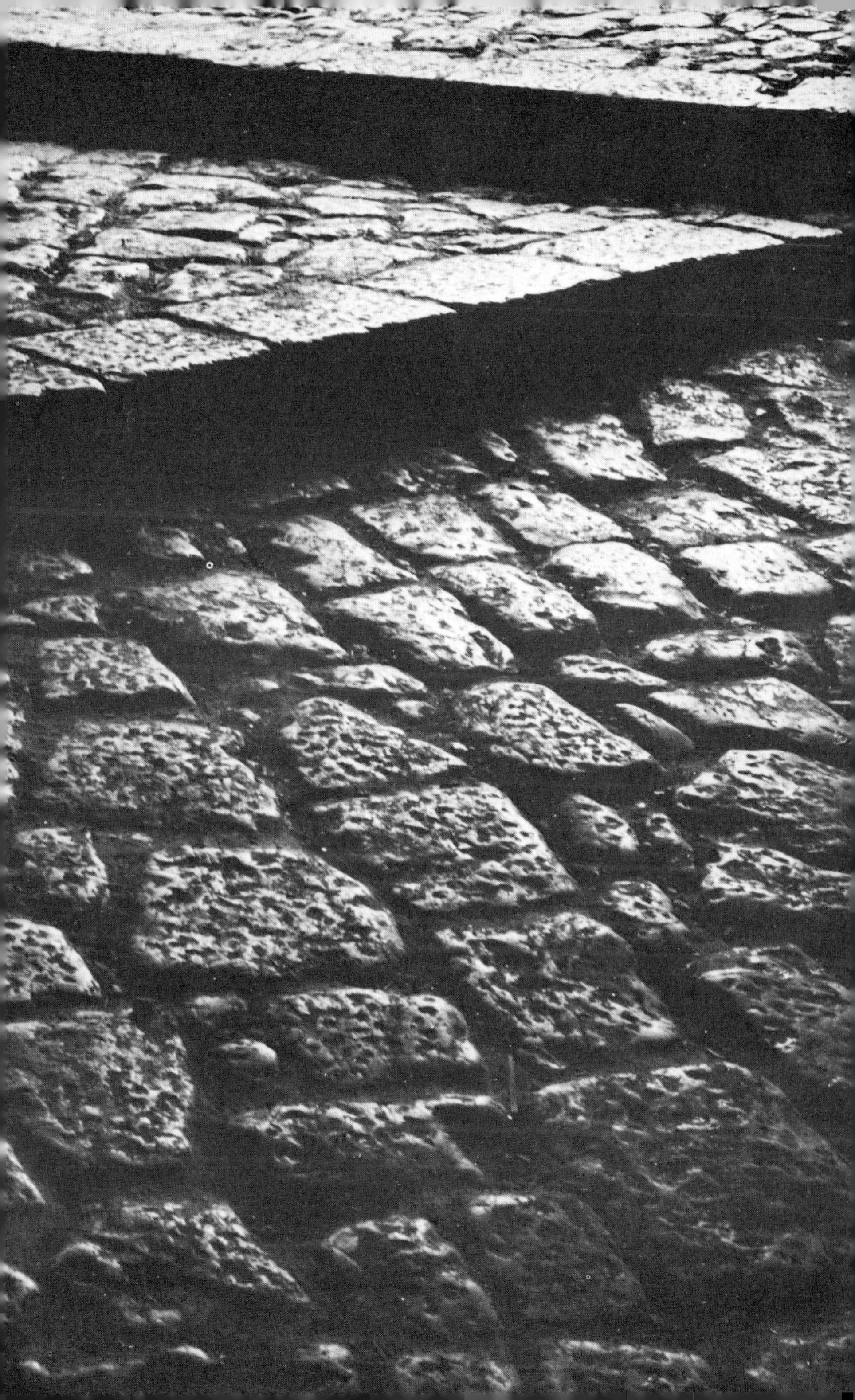

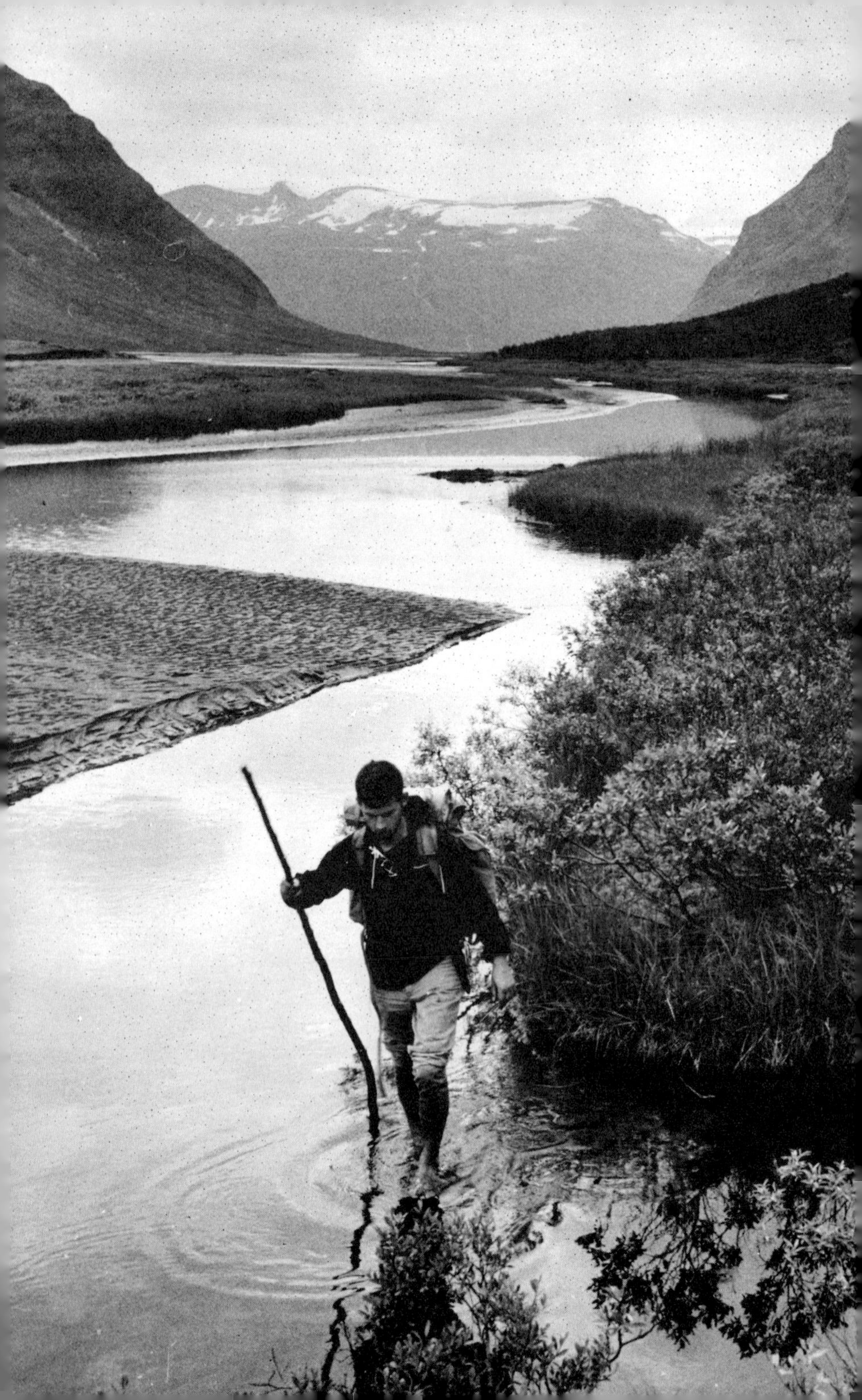

I will arise and go now, and go to Innisfree,
And a small cabin build there, of clay and
   wattles made;
Nine bean rows will I have there, a hive for
   the honey bee,
     And live alone in the bee-loud glade.

And I shall have some peace there, for peace
   comes dropping slow,
Dropping from the veils of the morning to
   where the cricket sings;
There midnight's all a-glimmer, and noon
   a purple glow,
     And evening full of the linnet's wings.

I will arise and go now, for always night and day
I hear lake water lapping with low sounds
   by the shore;
While I stand on the roadway, or on the
   pavements gray,
     I hear it in the deep heart's core.

               William Butler Yeats

Traveling with me you find what never tires.
The earth never tires,
The earth is rude, silent, incomprehensible at first,
    Nature is rude and incomprehensible at first,
Be not discouraged, keep on, there are divine things
    well envelop'd,
I swear to you there are divine things
    more beautiful than words can tell.

                      Walt Whitman

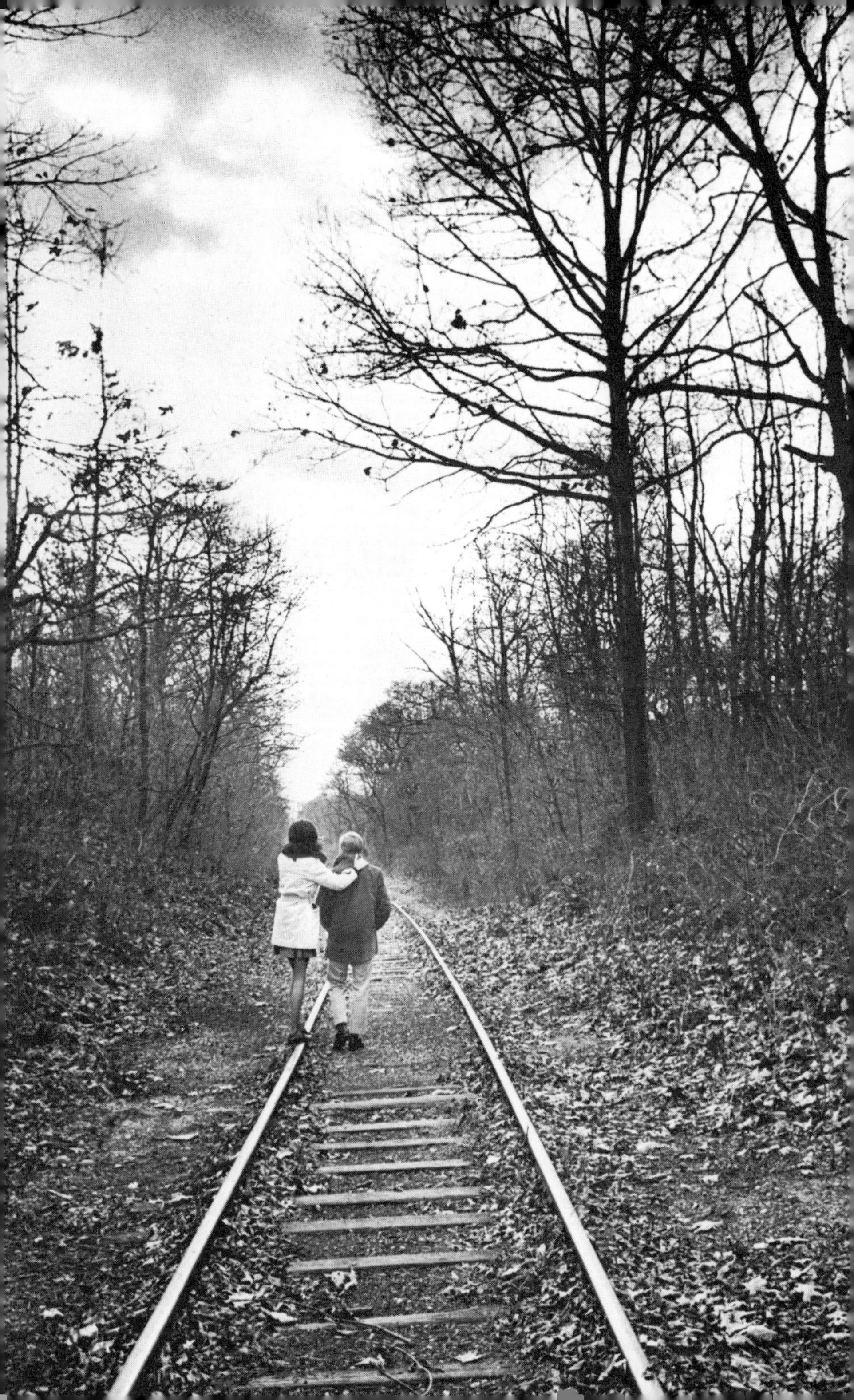

Now I could wish at once to sleep,
To fall asleep in moonlit dark,
'Mid sounds of foliage whispering deep,
Sparks in my blood, each leaf a spark,
Hearing a melody strange and new—
The clock strikes two.

      Annette Von Droste-Hülshoff

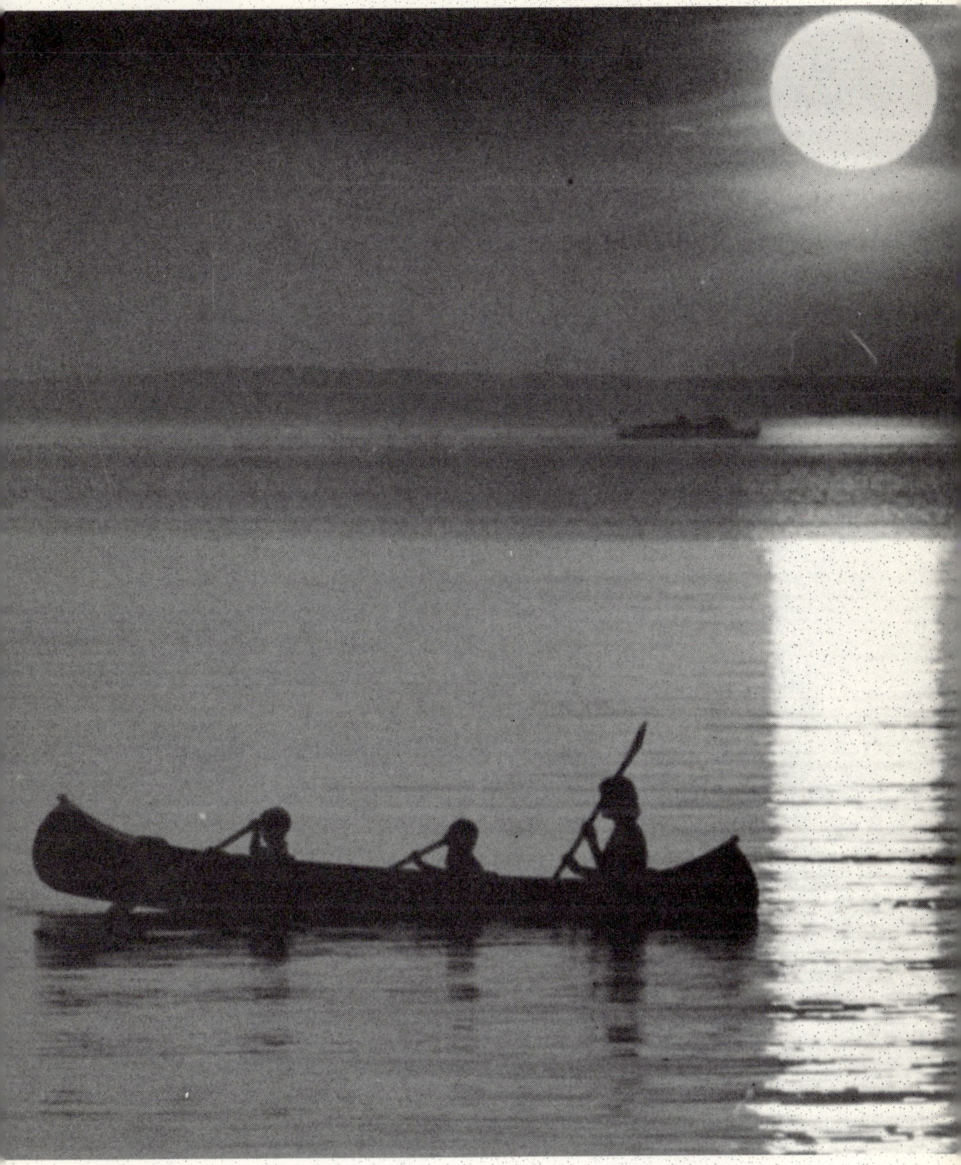

EXPERIENCING THINGS

Get to know nature. Run and roll in it. Swim and shiver in it. Whatever you do, get into it. All the way. Don't hold back. Experience it all together. You and everything around you can become a single, pulsating organism. "You are," as Alan Watts says, "both the leaf and the wind." Enter every experience with every needed sense alert. Let it happen to you. Fully.

The world is so full
　　　of a number of things,
I'm sure we should all
　　　be as happy as kings.

Robert Louis Stevenson

Climb the mountains
and get their
good tidings.
Nature's peace
will flow into you
as sunshine flows
into trees.
The winds will blow
their own freshness
into you,
and the storms
their energy,
while cares
will drop away
from you
like the leaves
of Autumn.

      John Muir

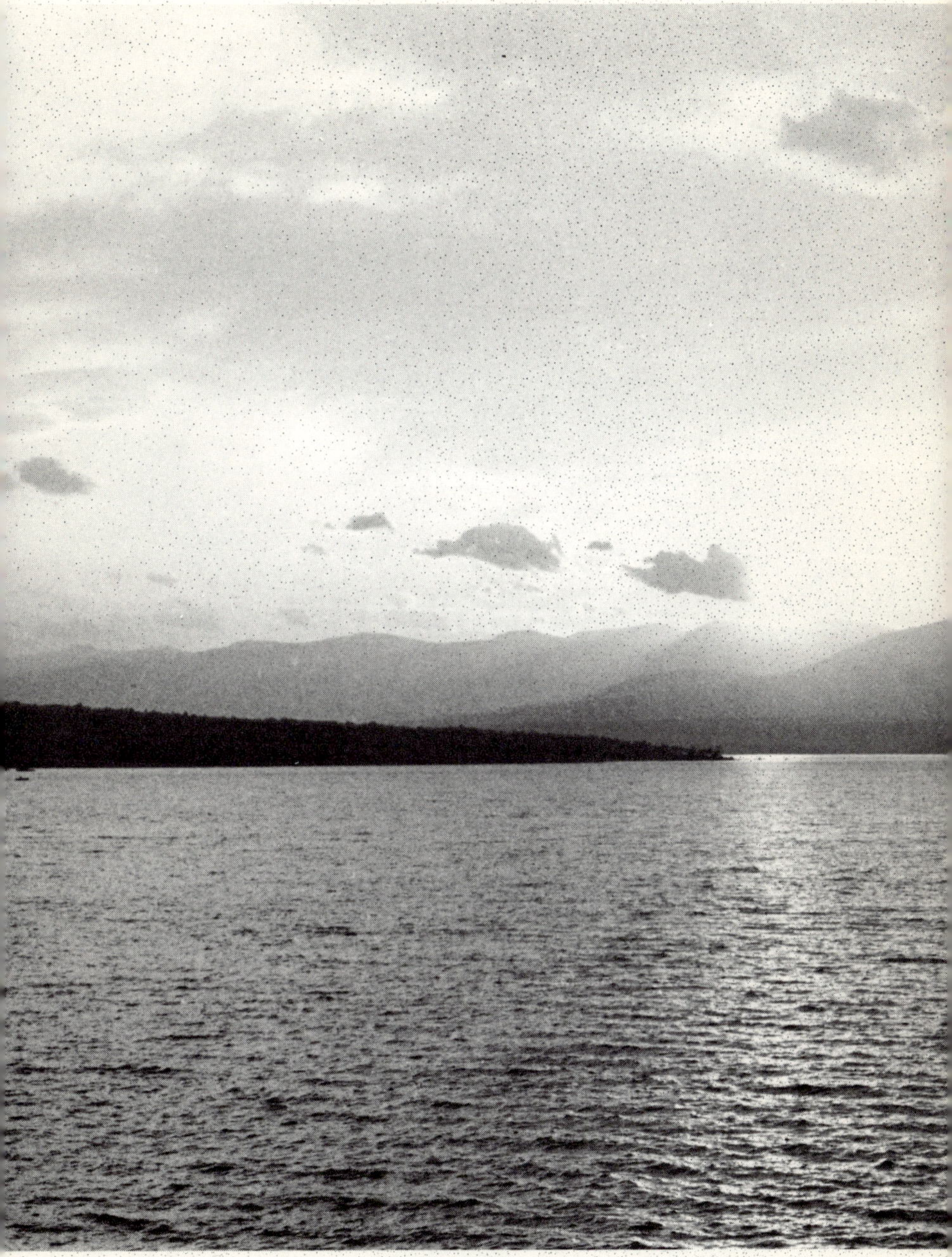

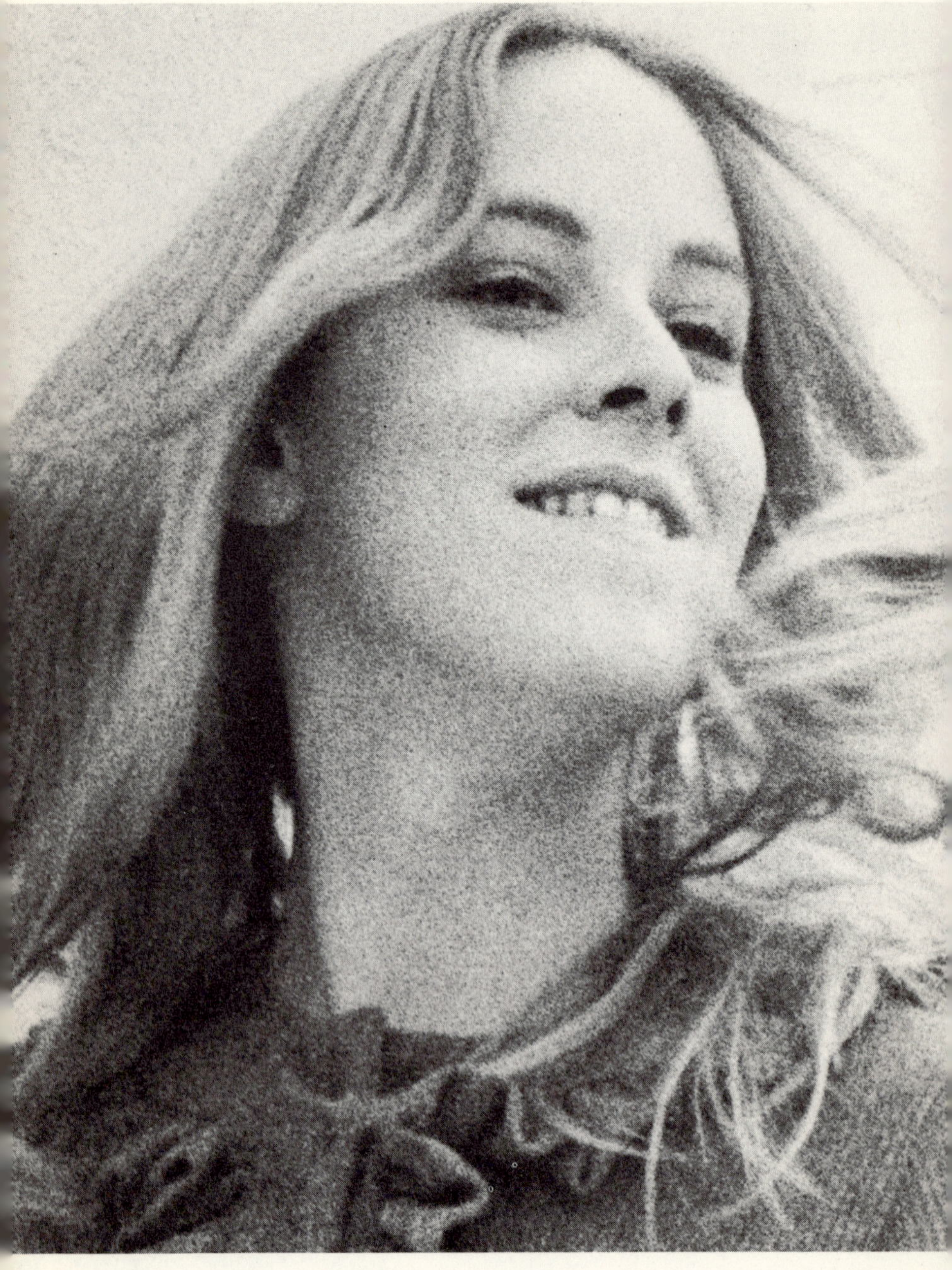

Roaring Wind, soaring Wind,
Leaping the skies,
Tell me where your homeland lies.

"Child, we've been blowing
Years, years beyond all knowing
Round the wide, the wide old world,
That same question crying,
Demanding a replying,
Asking the mountains, seas, and coasts,
Asking the heaven's sounding hosts,
And not one could say!
If you're wiser than they
We would learn it of you!
But onward, away!
Bid us not stay!
Behind us there are coming others,
Ask our brothers!"

    Edward Mörike

Stodgily
the commuter train
moves ahead
rickety, rattling
    at each stop.

But I
pause to glance
    at a passing lake,
and to watch
morning haze
    rise and reveal
reflecting pink clouds
and faint sunrise
    unveiling
a crystal autumn
    day.

        Alice Sullivan

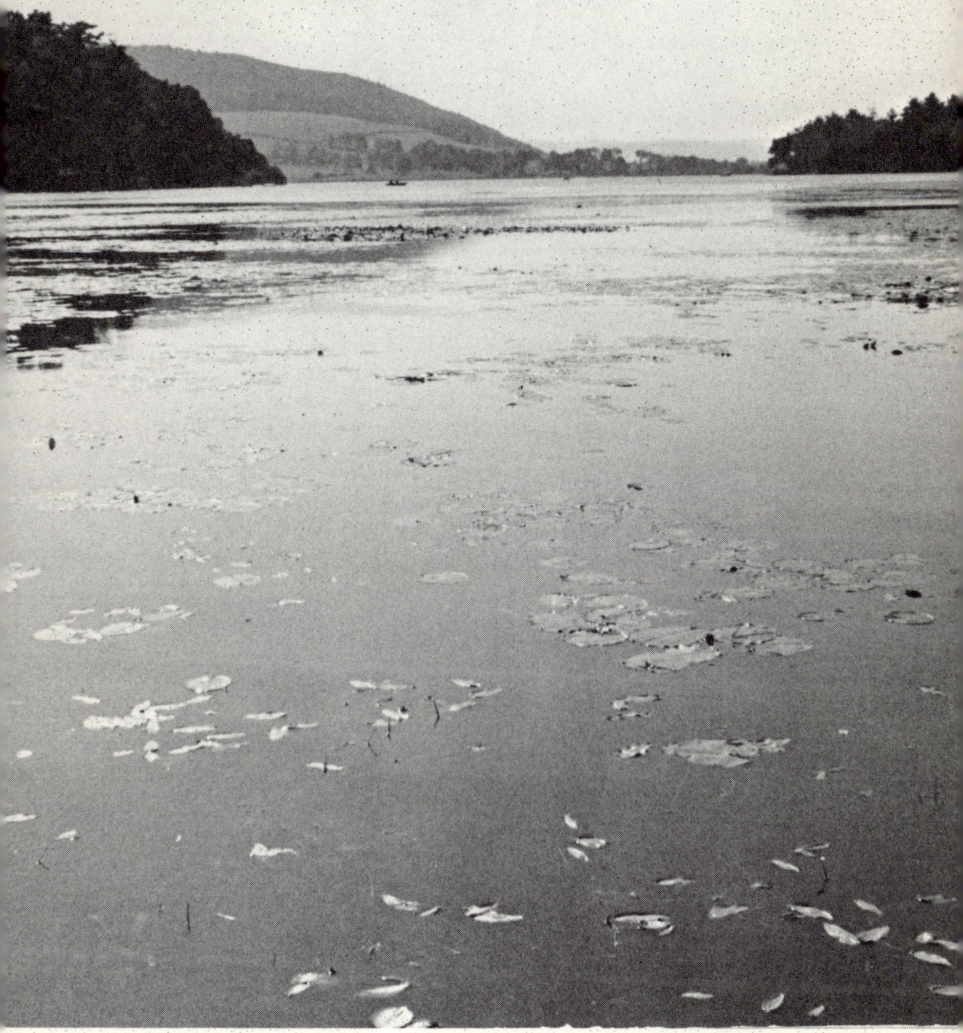

THE UNIVERSE IS ALIVE AND READY

The universe is alive and it belongs to you. It was made for you to live in and love. If you don't enjoy it, then to that degree it will fail to be an integral part of your life. If you restrain your feelings toward the universe, then to that degree you limit your own freedom. Take the leap.

Evening had fallen when he woke
and the sand and the arid grasses
of his bed glowed no longer.
He rose slowly and,
recalling the rapture of his sleep,
sighed at its joy.

He climbed to the crest
of the sandhill
and gazed about him.
Evening had fallen.
A rim of the young moon cleft
the pale waste of skyline,
the rim of a silver hoop
embedded in grey sand;
and the tide was flowing in fast
to the land
with a low whisper
of her waves,
islanding a few
last figures
in distant pools.

                    James Joyce

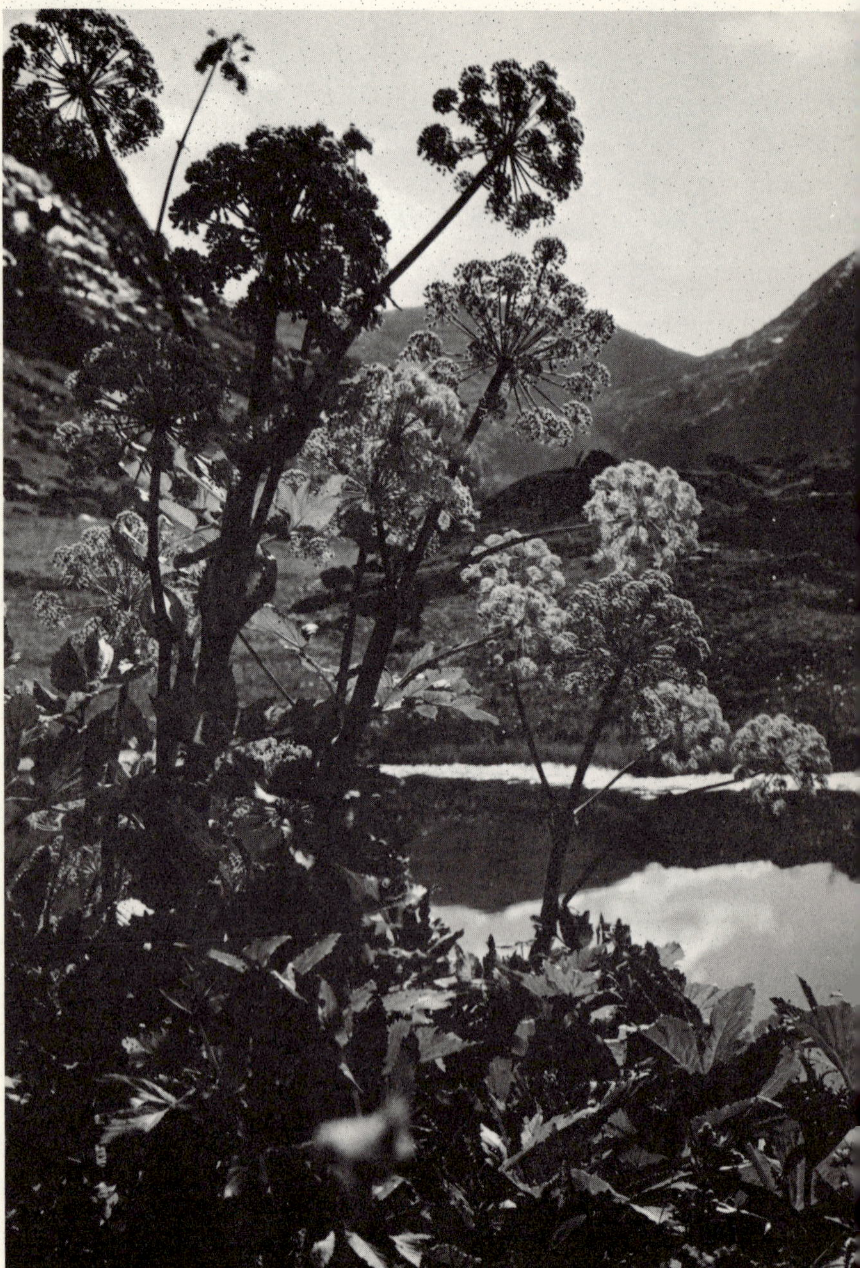

Flowers have an expression
of countenance
as much as men or animals.
Some seem to smile;
some have a sad expression;
some are pensive and diffident;
others again are plain,
honest and upright,
like the broadfaced sunflower
and the hollyhock.

    Henry Ward Beecher

My garden, with its silence
and the pulses of fragrance
that come and go
on the airy undulations,
affects me like sweet music.
Care stops at the gates,
and gazes at me wistfully
through the bars.
Among my flowers and trees,
Nature takes me into her own hands,
and I breathe freely as the first man.

    Alexander Smith

Man, free thinker! do you believe
that you alone think in this world
where life bursts forth in everything? ...
Your freedom has power
to use the strength you possess,
but the universe is absent
from all your councils.

   Gérard De Nerval

   Come! The sun speaks to you
   in sublime words;
   be endlessly absorbed
   in its relentless flame;
   and return with slow steps
   towards the abject cities,
   your heart seven times bathed.
   in the divine void.

      Leconte De Lisle

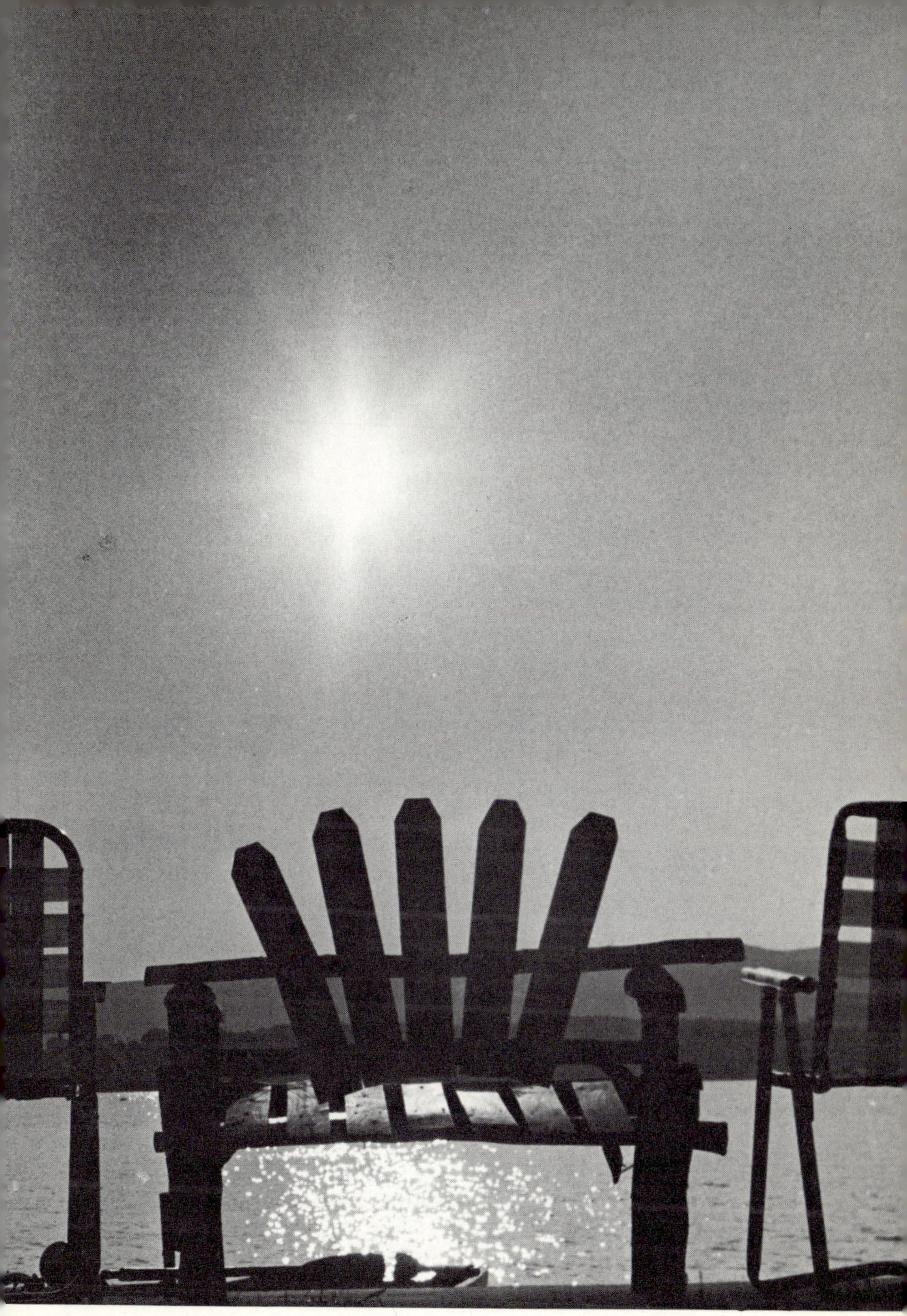

The spring that brims and ripples oh I know
    in dark of night.

Waters that flow forever and a day
through a lost country—oh I know the way
    in dark of night.

Its origin no knowing, for there's none.
But well I know, from here all sources run
    in dark of night.

     John of the Cross

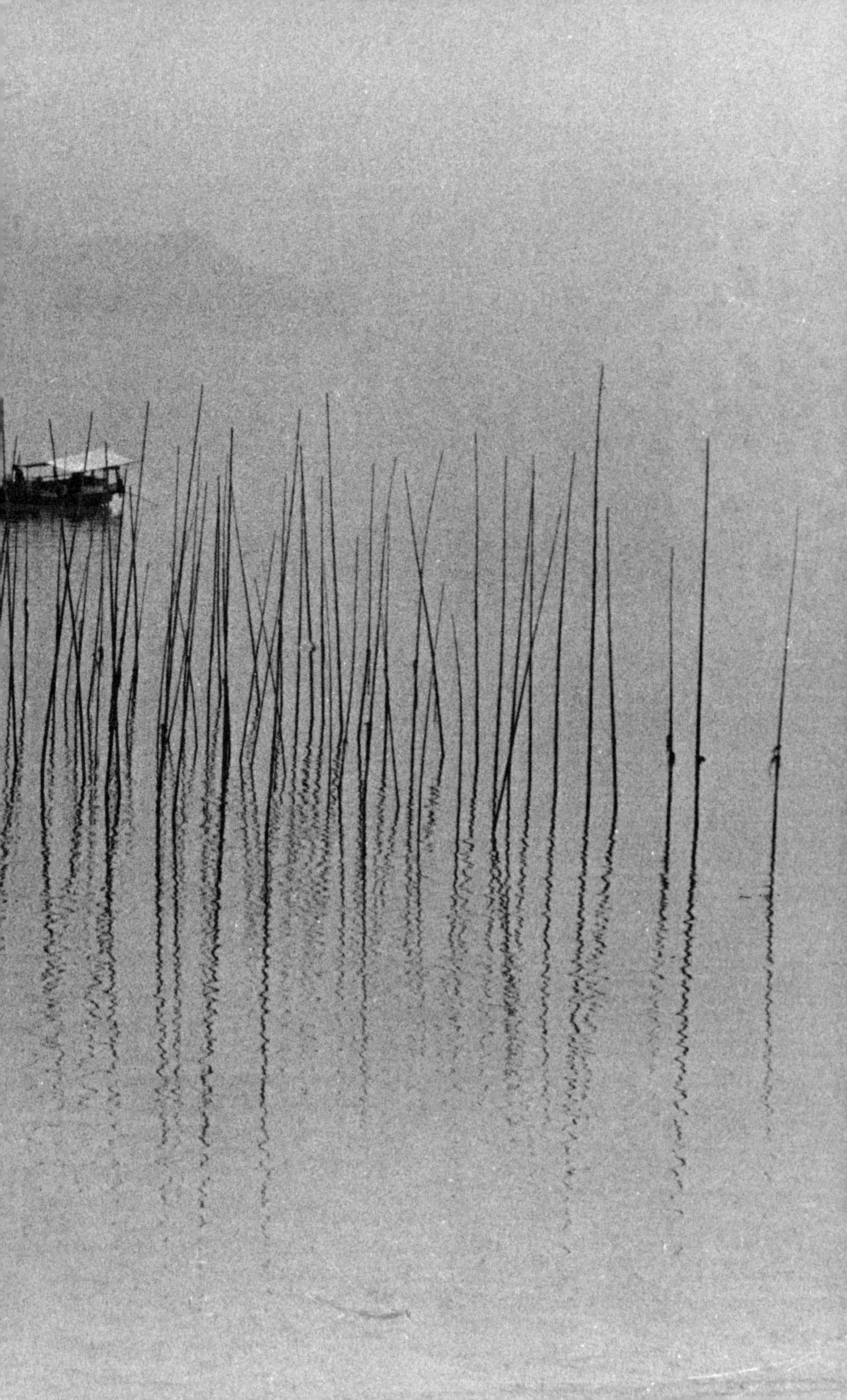

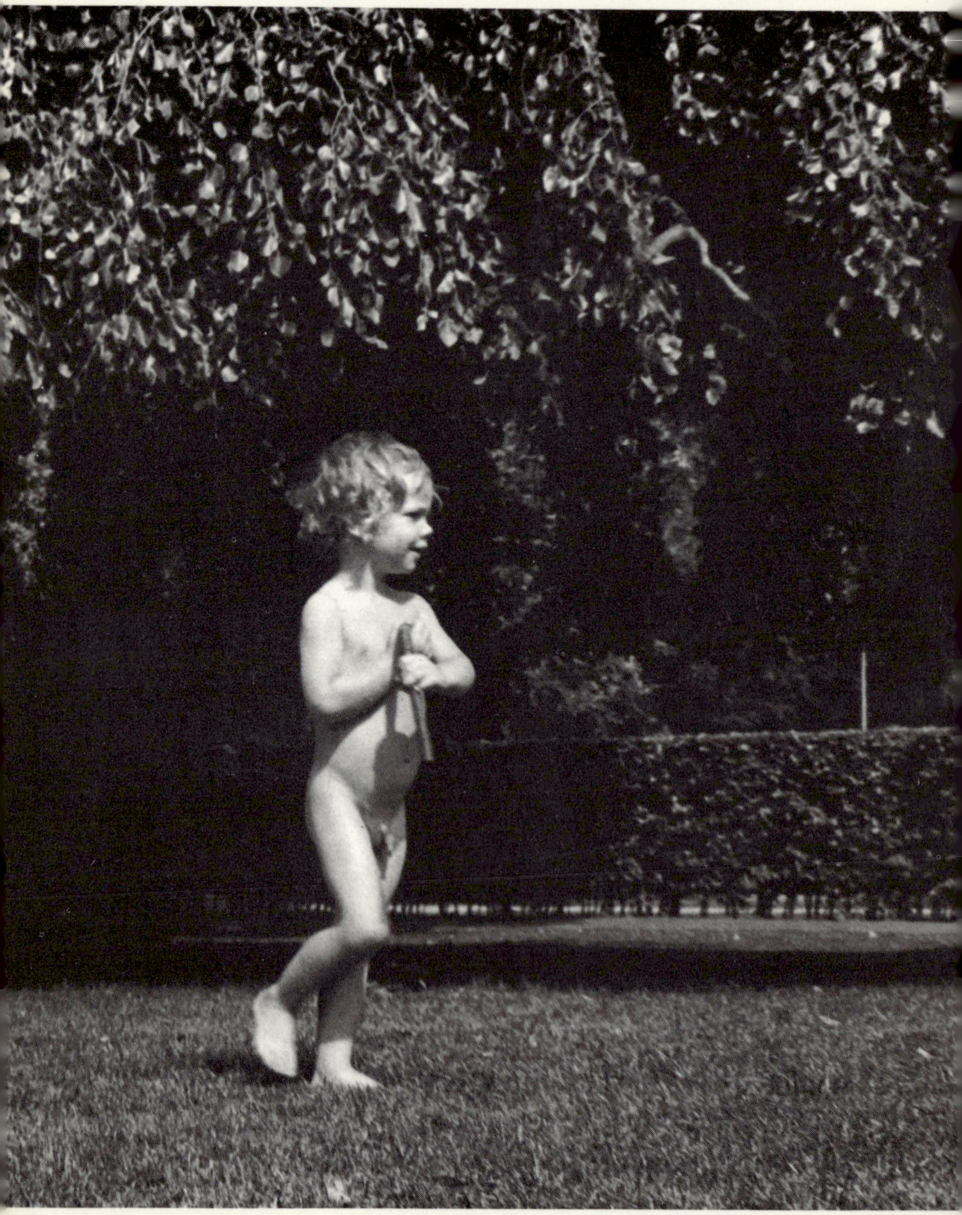

MY BODY IN THE UNIVERSE

"People are just as wonderful as sunsets," says psychologist Carl Rogers. The human body is where we first watch the gradual unfolding of life. As a healthy and vibrant body can enhance the experience of living in joy, so a "pained, tired, deadened, or unfeeling body cannot experience itself fully," writes psychologist William Schutz. A person's body is the one vast gateway to the natural high experience—almost as wide as the universe itself.

To find the kingdom in one's own body,
and to find one's own body
in the outside world.
The body to be realized
is the body of the cosmic man,
the body of the universe
as one perfect man.

        Norman O. Brown

What happens to the person's own body...
is identical with what happens in the universe.

        Jean Daniélou

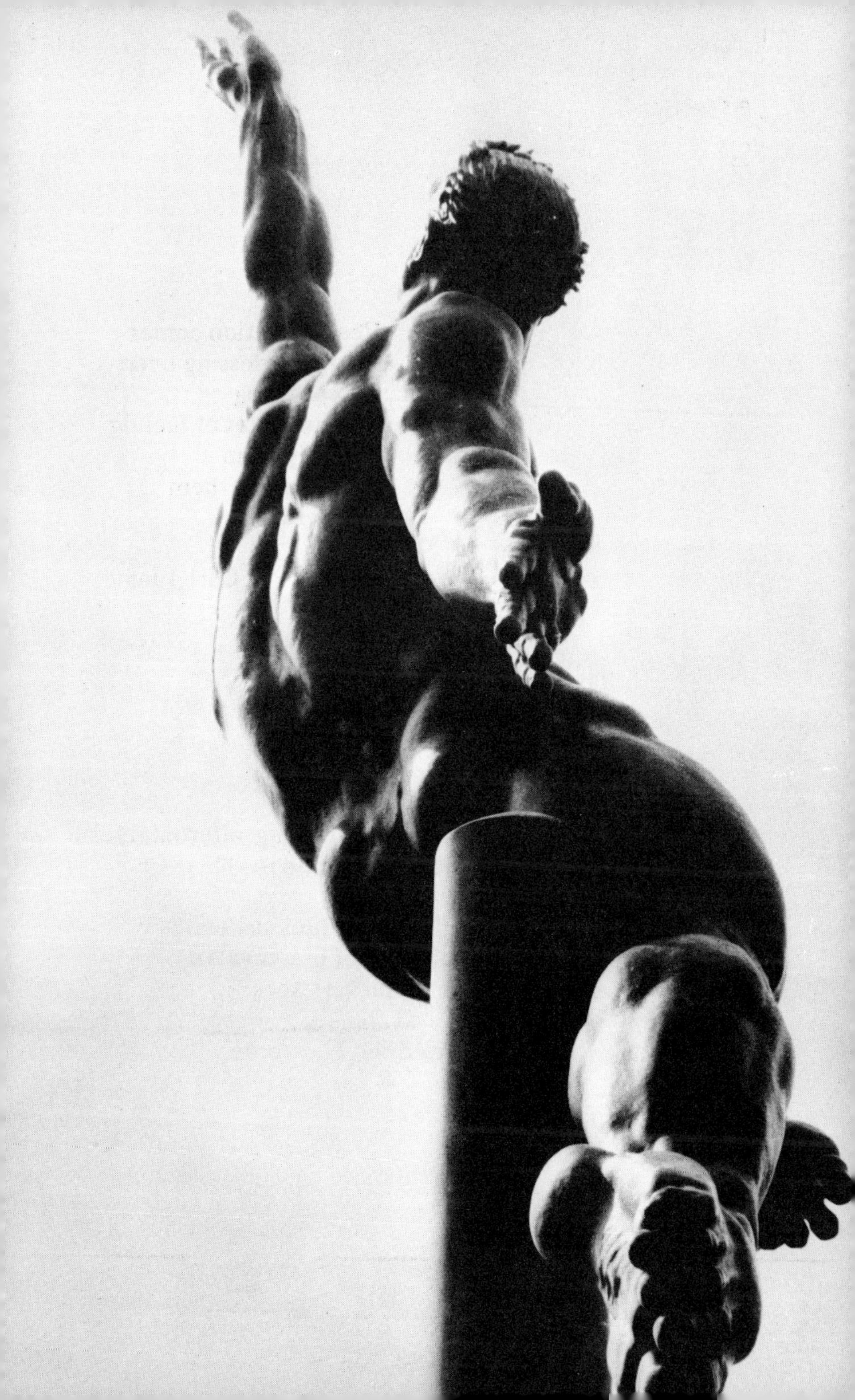

**Real liberation comes
not from glossing over
or repressing
painful states of feeling,
but only from
experiencing them
to the full.**

                Carl Jung

There is an ecstasy
such that the immense strain of it
is sometimes relaxed
by a flood of tears,
along with which one's steps
either rush or involuntarily lag, alternately.
There is the feeling that one is
completely out of hand,
with the very distinct consciousness
of an endless number of fine thrills
and quiverings to the very toes.

                Friedrich Nietzsche

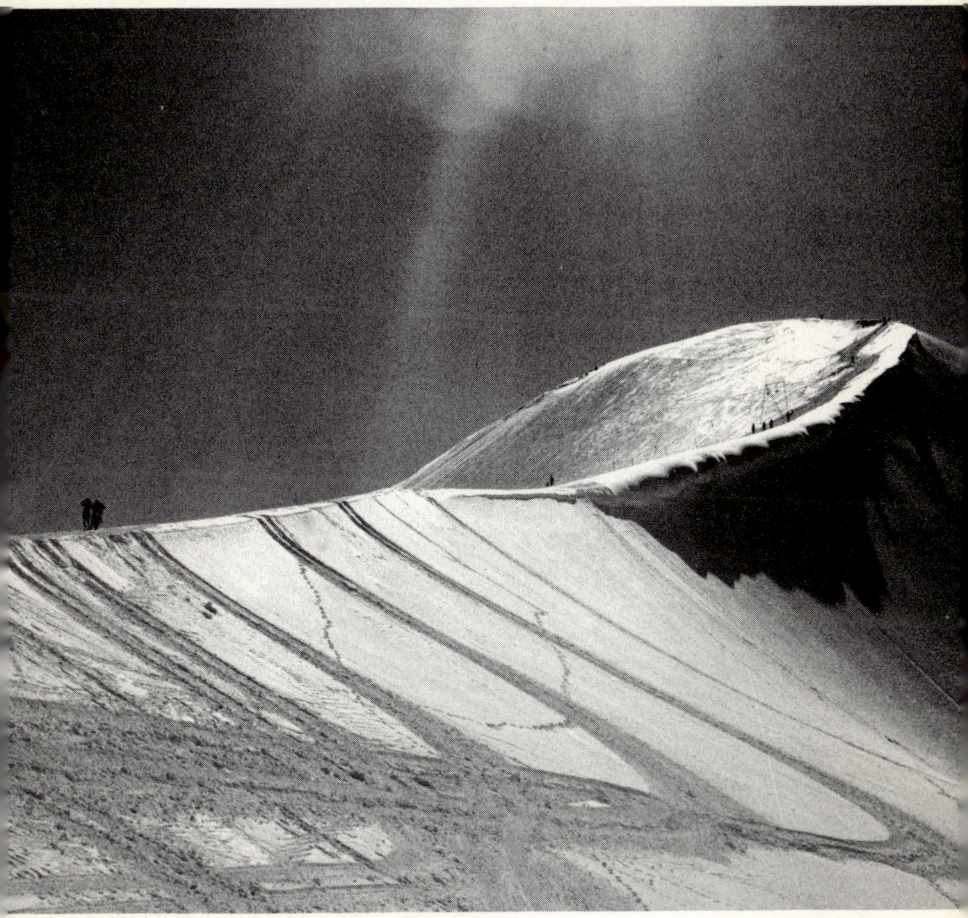

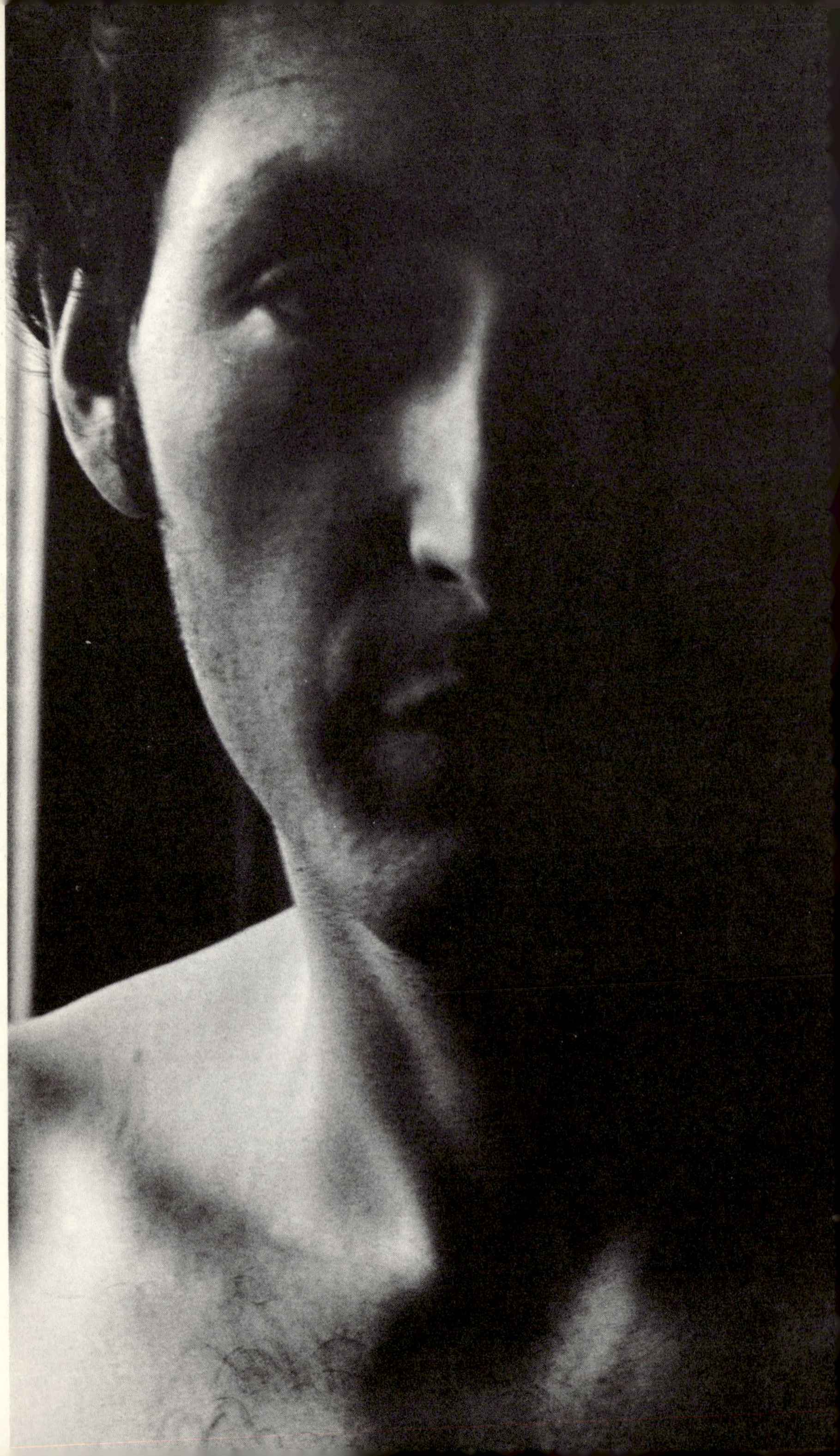

To the enlightened man,
whose consciousness
embraces the universe,
to him the universe
becomes his body.

        A. Storch

MY SELF, UNIQUE AND ALONE

As you grow to know yourself, you will be less likely to place limitations on your potential to experience life. You will be constantly and repeatedly surprised at your new-found capacity to feel in ways you never predicted or never suspected. Even negative states of feeling—loneliness, sorrow, depression, or fear—can be explored with rich and positive human results.

A kind of waking trance
I have frequently had,
quite up from boyhood,
when I have been all alone.
This has generally come upon me
thro' repeating my own name
two or three times to myself silently,
till all at once,
as it were out of the intensity
of the consciousness of individuality,
the individuality itself seemed to dissolve
and fade away into boundless being,
and this not a confused state,
but the clearest of the clearest,
the surest of the surest,
the weirdest of the weirdest,
utterly beyond words,
where death was an almost
laughable impossibility,
the loss of personality (if so it were)
seeming no extinction
but the only true life.

        Alfred Lord Tennyson

We are not hen's eggs,
or bananas, or clothespins,
to be counted off by the dozen.
Down to the last detail
we are all different.
Everyone has his own fingerprints.
Recognize and rejoice
in that endless variety.
The white light of the divine purpose
streams down from heaven
to be broken up
by these human prisms
into all the colors of the rainbow.
Take your own color
in the pattern
and be just that.

     Charles R. Brown

I love to be alone.
I never found the companion
that was so companionable
as solitude.

Henry David Thoreau

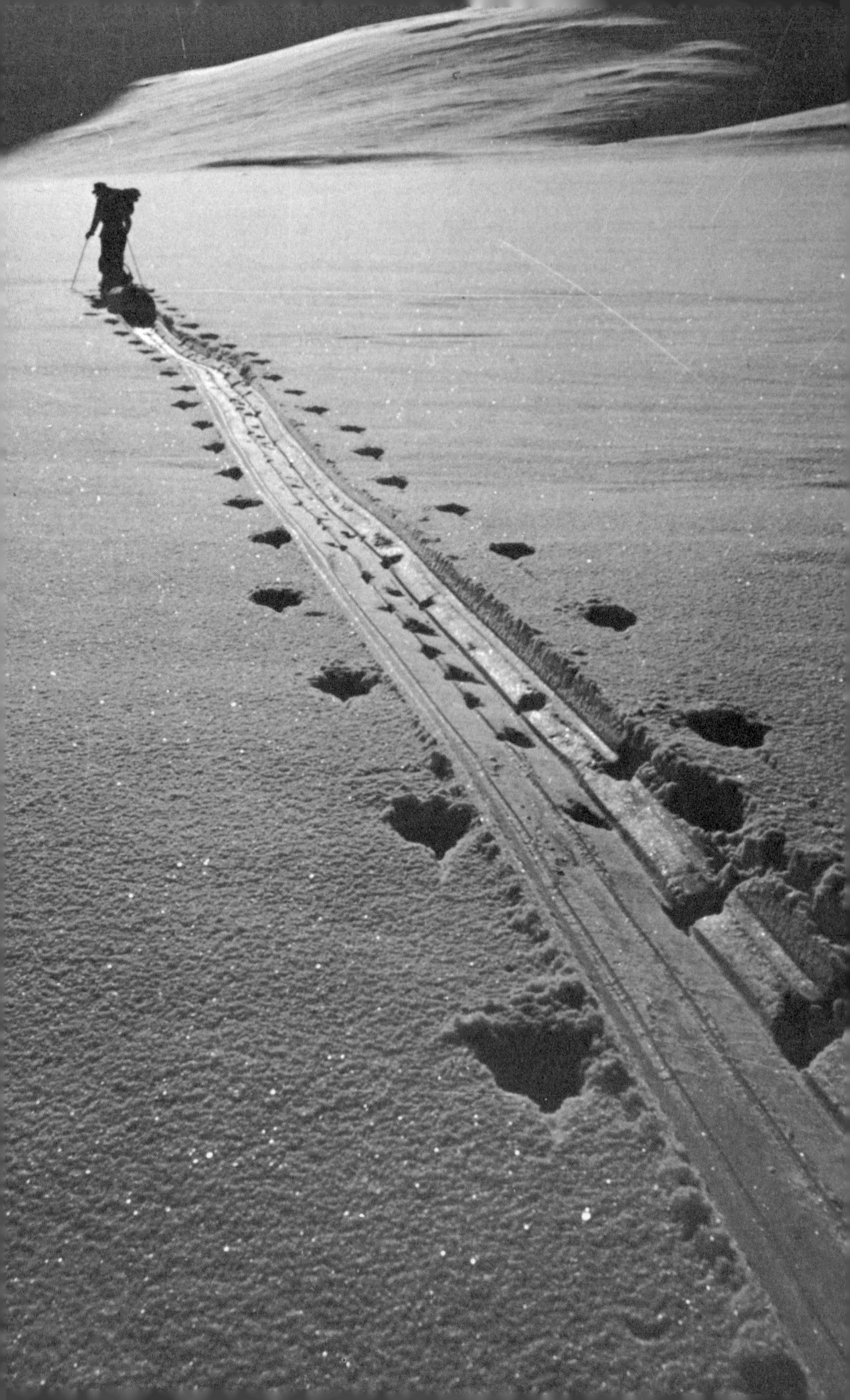

There is much evidence to show
that for anyone who passes
through the barrier of loneliness,
the sense of individual isolation bursts,
almost by dint of its own intensity,
into the "all-feeling" of identity with the universe.

Alan Watts

I AM MORE THAN MIND

If you could do no more than what your conscious attention allowed, you would have to do everything in succession. Life would be a single-file experience. Luckily, you can experience many things at once. Your body alone represents a complex set of organized activities, all running smoothly without your being conscious of it. Every person around you, every thing—animate or inanimate—impinges upon your consciousness, directly or so subtly that you rarely are aware of it. And you react—deliberately, knowingly, or unwittingly. To become more and more aware of the spontaneous things happening within and outside of you is to participate more fully in the dance of life.

There seems to be something phony
about every attempt to define myself,
to be totally honest.
The trouble is that I can't see the back,
much less the inside, of my head.
I can't be honest because
I don't fully know what I am.
Consciousness peers out from a center
which it cannot see—
and *that* is the root of the matter.

      Alan Watts

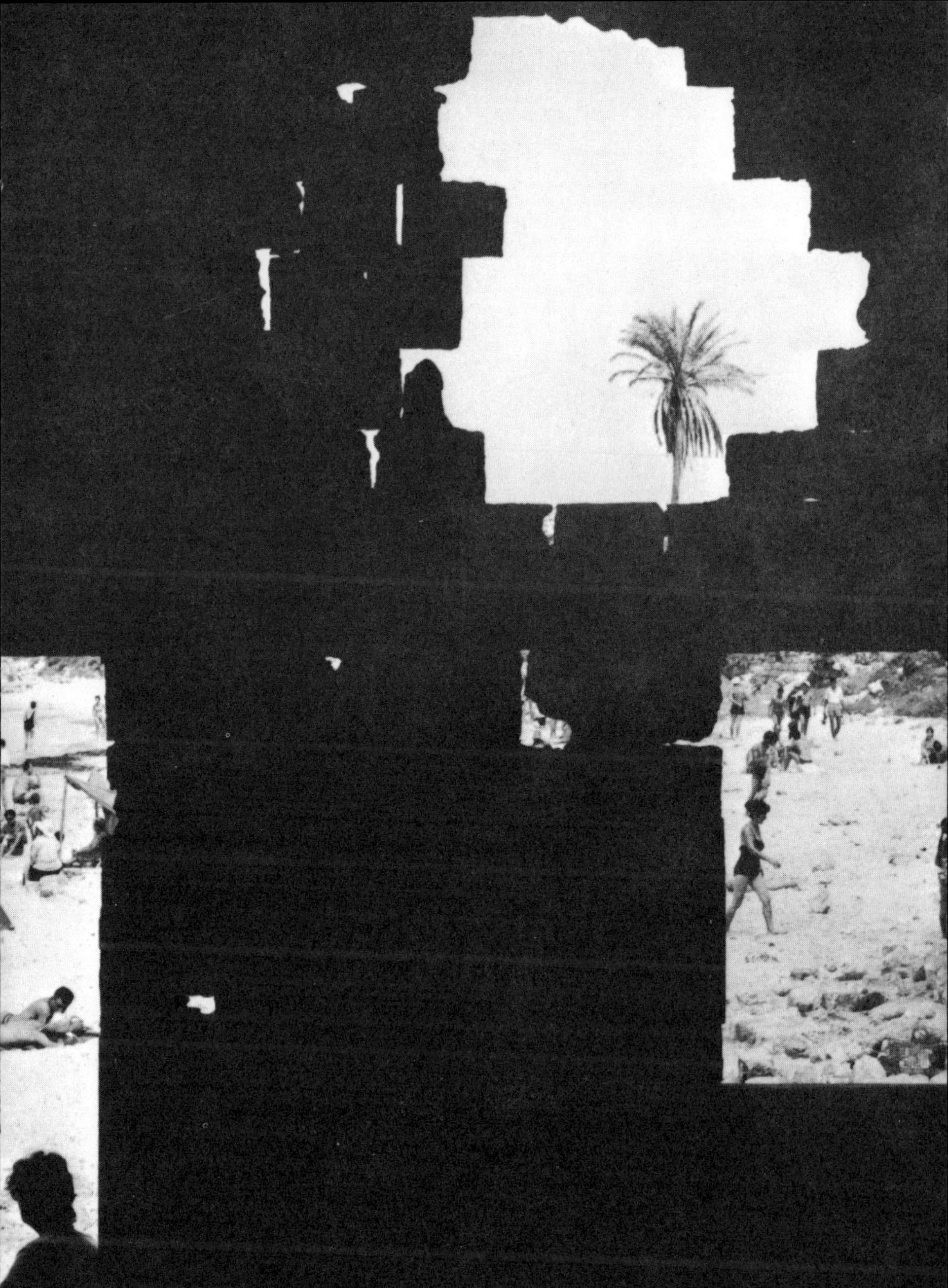

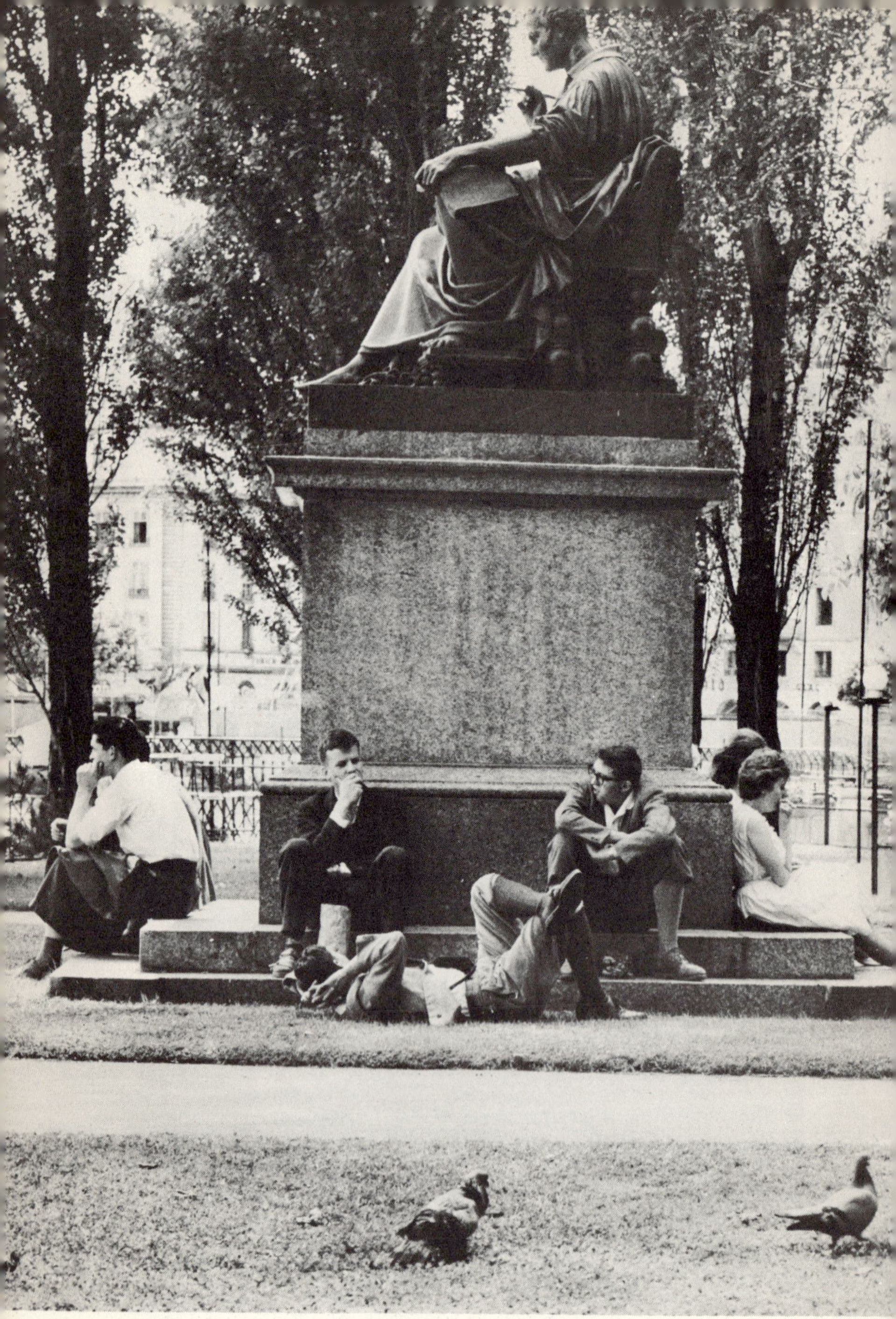

Knowledge seems more like
a kind of pain-killing drug
that I have to take repeatedly
against the boredom
and desolation of my heart.
And no matter how faithful
I may be to it,
it can never really cure me.

All it can give me
is words and concepts,
which perform the middleman's service
of expressing and interpreting
reality to me,
but can never still
my heart's craving
for the reality itself,
for true life and true possession.

I shall never be cured
until all reality
comes streaming like an ecstatic,
intoxicating melody
into my heart.

              Karl Rahner

Reason is only part of a man;
when it usurps most of one's living space
it becomes a tumor...
a cancer gnawing away
the other parts of human nature.

            John Langdon-Davies

If you wish to tranquilize your mind
and restore its original purity,
you must proceed as you would do
if you were purifying a jar of muddy water.
You first let it stand,
until the sediment settles at the bottom,
when the water will become clear,
which corresponds with the state of the mind
before it was troubled by defiling passions.
Then you carefully strain off the pure water...
When the mind becomes tranquilized
and concentrated into perfect unity,
then all things will be seen,
not in their separateness,
but in their unity, wherein there is
no place for the passions to enter,
and which is in full conformity
with the mysterious and indescribable
purity of Nirvana.

     Surangama Sutra

I do my utmost to attain emptiness;
I hold firmly to stillness.
The myriad creatures all rise together
And I watch their return.
The teeming creatures
All return to their separate roots.
Returning to one's roots is known as stillness.
This is what is meant by returning to one's destiny.

     Lao Tzu

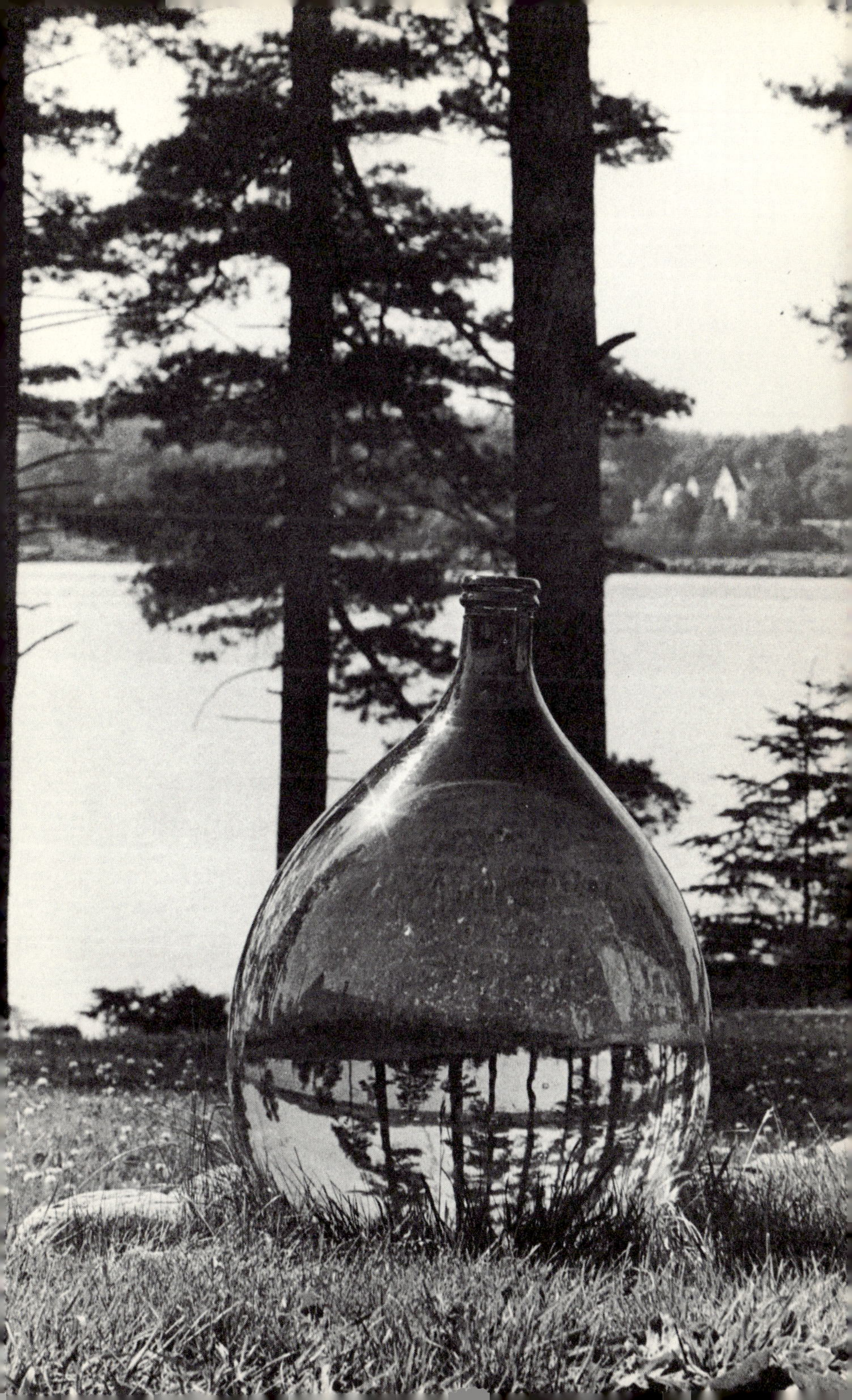

TRANSFORMATION

To function fully and properly, to have body, mind and spirit all together, it is not enough to simply reorder your thoughts. More than a change of attitude, you must also allow your organism to live freely. When the total organism becomes self-controlling instead of self-frustrating, only then can you begin to live higher and higher.

Fulfillment brings to an individual
the feeling that he can cope
with his environment;
the sense of confidence in himself
as a significant, competent, lovable person
who is capable of handling situations as they arise,
able to use fully his own capacities,
and free to express his feelings.
Joy requires a vital, alive body, self-contentment,
productive and satisfying relations with others,
and a successful relation to society.

            William C. Schutz

Reality
and the addiction
to any one reality
is a tissue-thin
neurological fragility.
At the height
of a visionary experience
it is crystal-clear
that you can change
completely.

        Timothy Leary

Can you walk on water?
You have done no better
than a straw.
Can you fly in the air?
You have done no better
than a bluebottle.
Conquer your heart;
then you may become somebody.

        Ansari of Herat

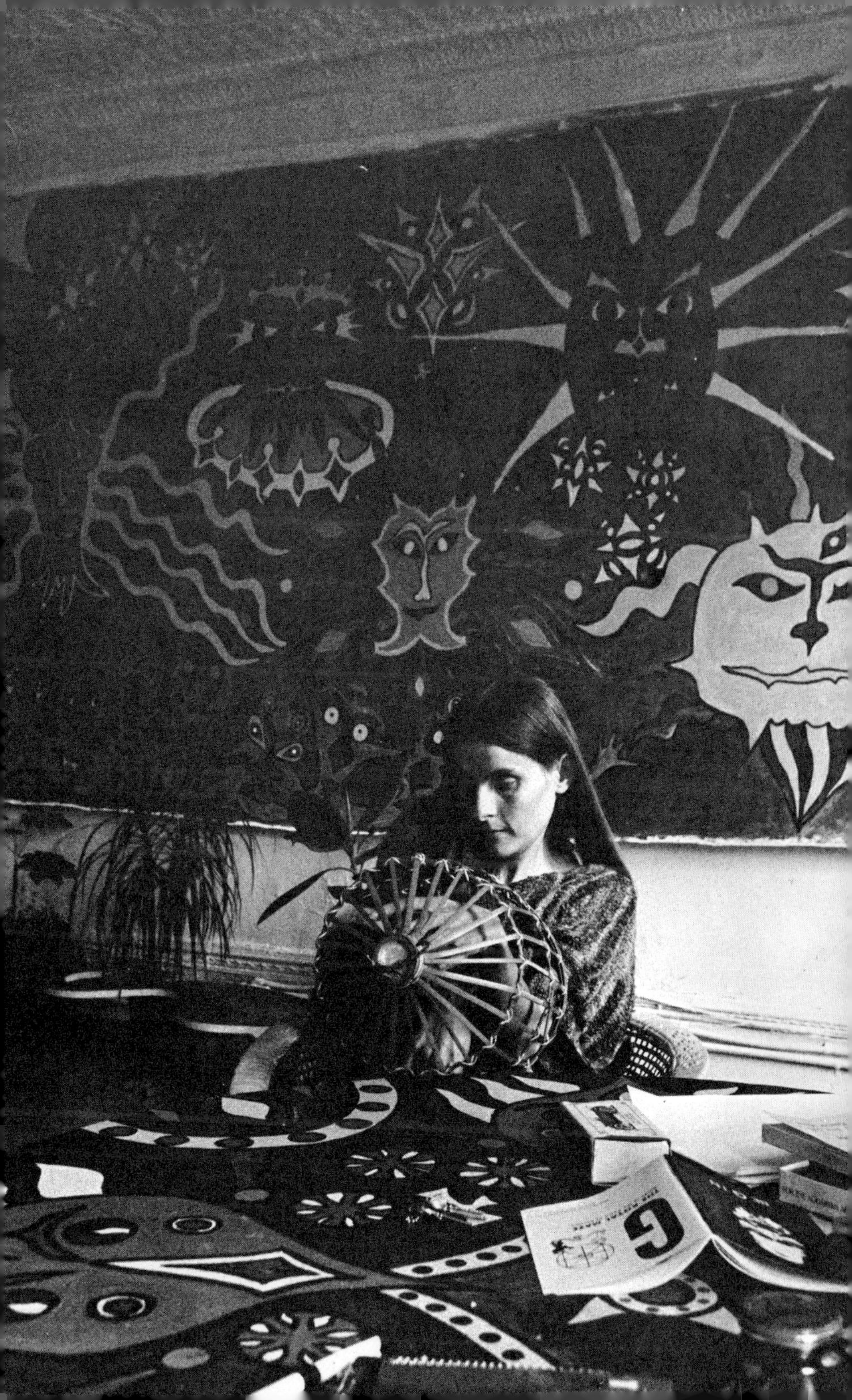

Every means to the end of growth
should itself be outgrown.
When the growth has been achieved,
the means should be discarded,
as is the scaffolding
used to erect a building.
One may use a raft to cross a stream,
but he is handicapped
if he tries to carry it on his shoulders
as he explores the other shore.

                John W. Aiken

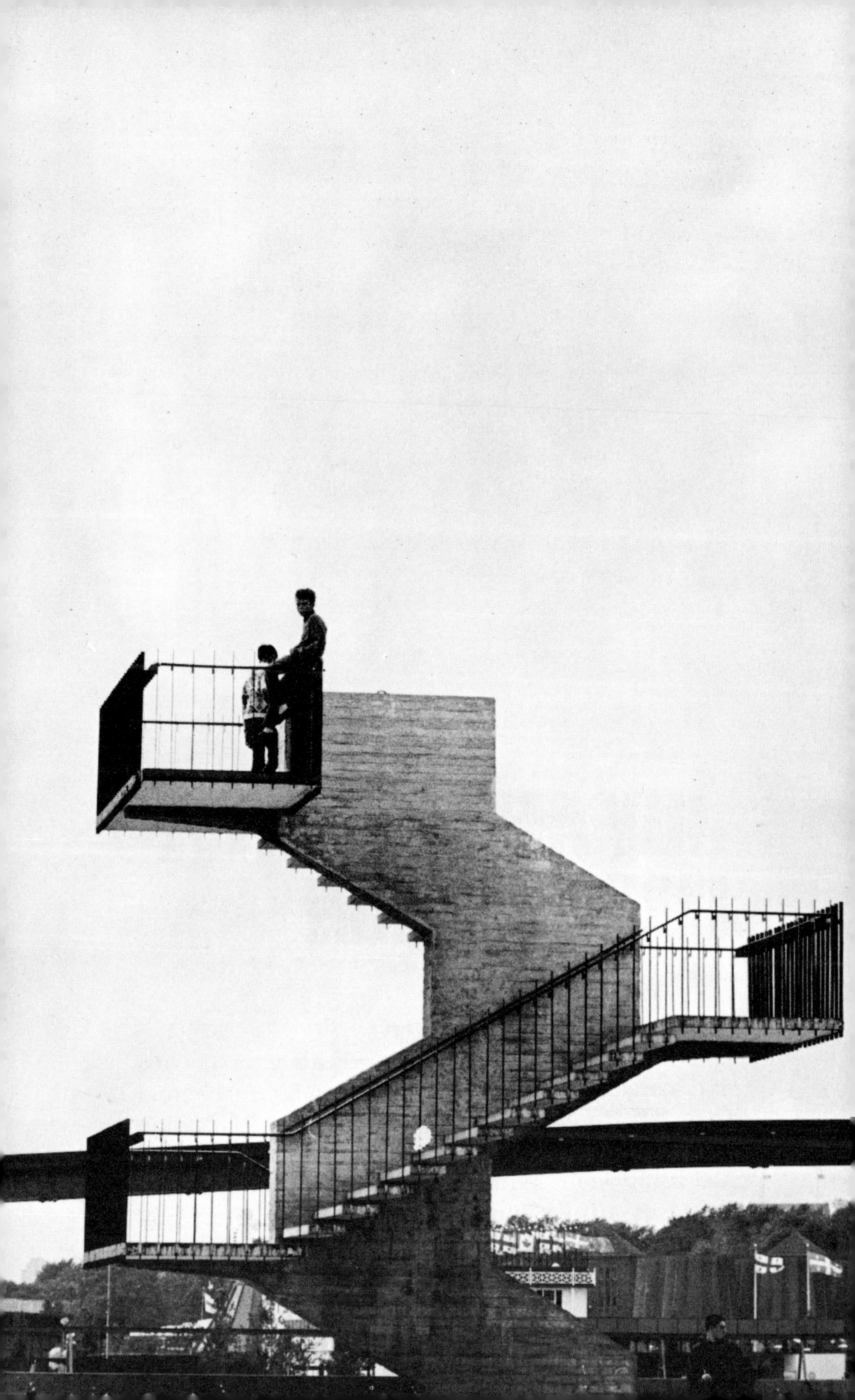

JOY AND CREATIVE IMAGINATION

Creativity implies the full use of all your powers and capacities, but it can also lead you beyond them into previously unexplored areas of human experience. Joy is the unmistakable sign that you are using your mind creatively and that you are living as a fully functioning person. In short, joy tells you that you are alive, really alive.

Man's capacities have never been measured;
nor are we to judge of what he can do
by any precedents, so little has been tried.

Henry David Thoreau

One of the strongest incentives
to human activity
and one of the oldest,
is the aesthetic sense
which awakens in man
the urge to create works of art
as well as to embark
upon scientific discovery;
the need to create a work of art,
like the need to investigate
and understand the mysteries of nature,
both originate, in varying degrees,
in the desire to achieve
that balance and harmony
through which man seeks
to rise above himself.

              Jean-Jacques Trillat

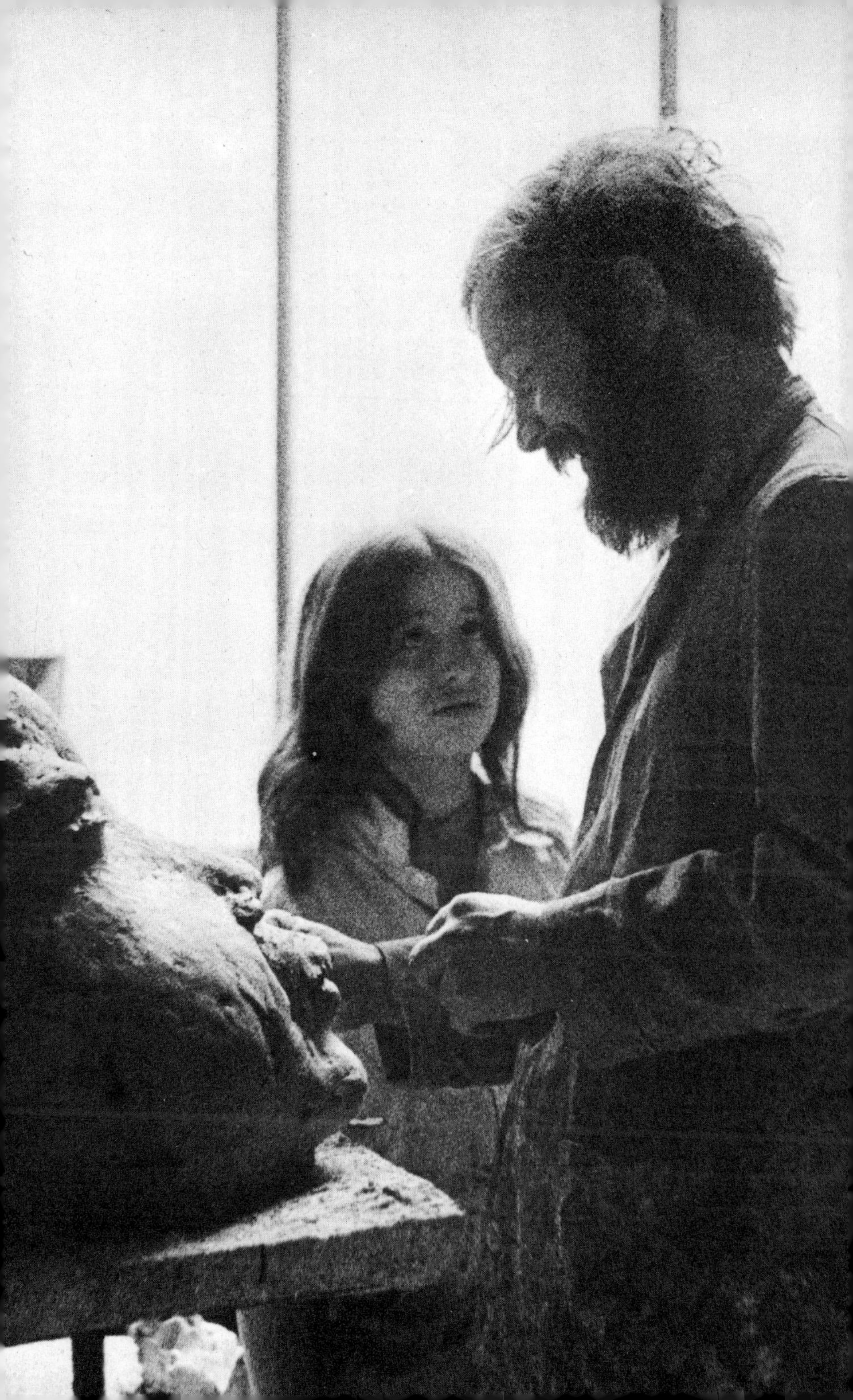

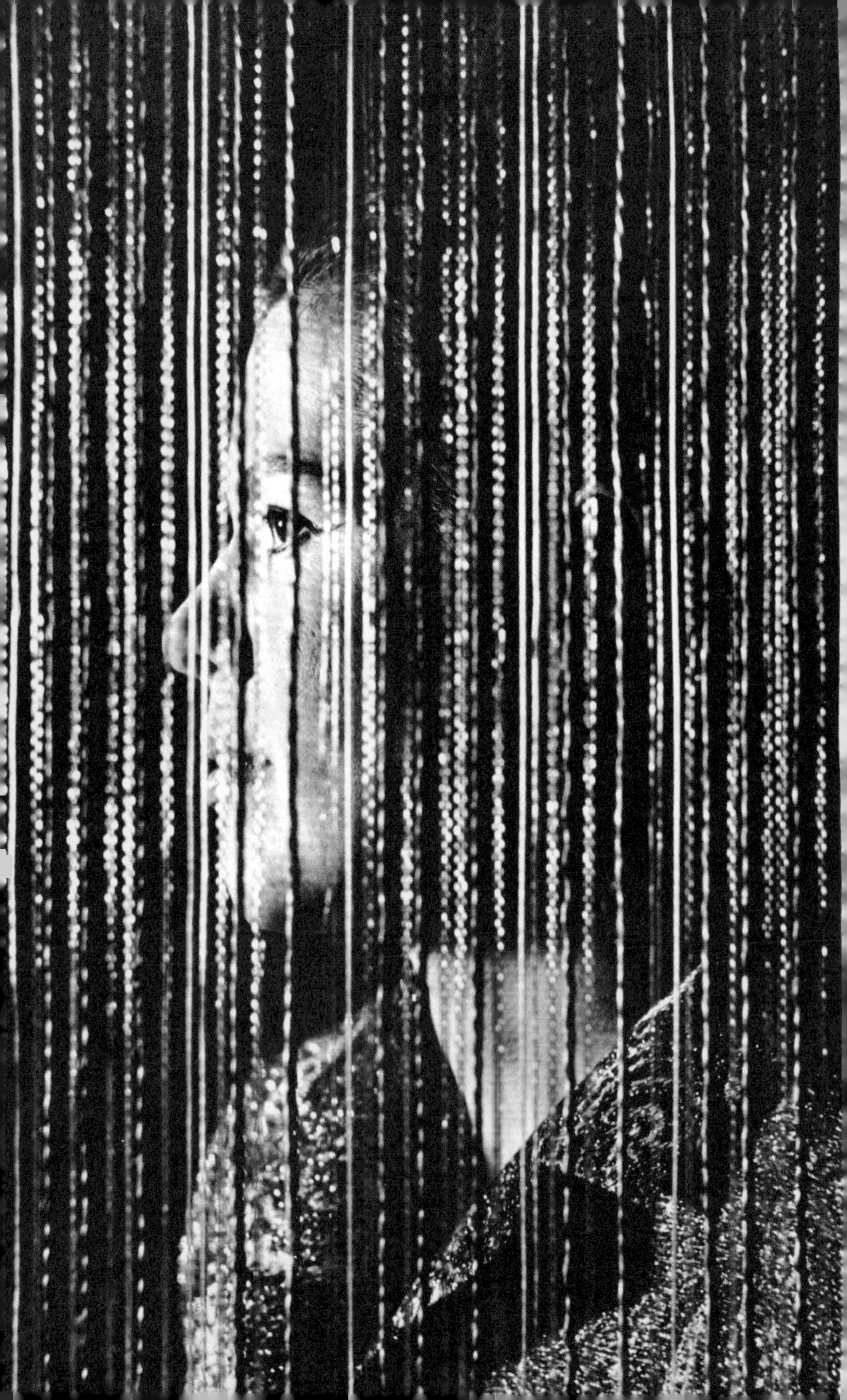

The manner in which
one single ray of light,
one single precious hint,
will clarify and energize
the whole mental life
of him who receives it,
is among the most wonderful
and heavenly of intellectual phenomena.

    Arnold Bennett

    The notion of revelation
    describes the conditions
    quite simply;
    by which I mean
    that something profoundly
    convulsive and disturbing
    suddenly becomes visible
    and audible ...
    One hears—one does not seek;
    one takes—one does not ask who gives;
    a thought flashes out like lightning.

        Friedrich Nietzsche

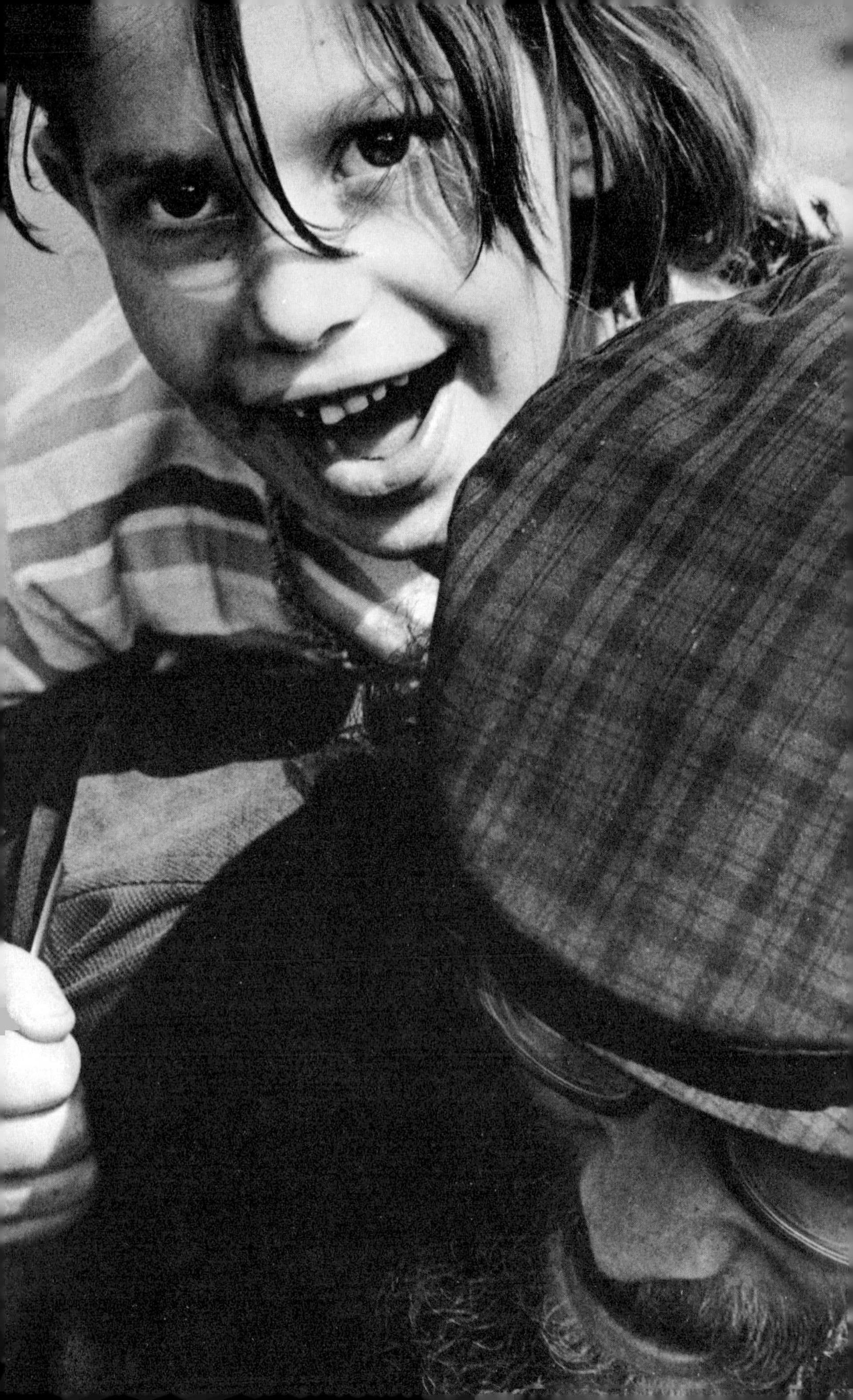

FREEDOM AND THE FUTURE

Everyone wants to be real, authentic, himself or herself. When you explore what you are in a fully aware manner—your pain and labor and sweat as well as your joy and play and laughter — you can learn to see yourself as a new person, being born again each new day, singing a new song. Those who know this newness have no fear of growing old.

Building a life is the finest of all arts.
Many people have sufficient information
about the facts of life,
but few know how to really live.
Since the individual is, to a great extent,
the architect of his own destiny,
he should waste no time
in getting his purposes
coordinated and associated
with a balanced personality,
where he can weave them all
into a harmonious pattern of life.
The sooner this is done
the more peace and happiness he can find.

        William H. McClurg

The basis of freedom
is recognition of the unconscious;
the invisible dimension;
the not yet realized;
leaving a space for the new.

        E. S. Morgan

The unconscious to be made conscious;
a secret disclosed;
a veil to be rent,
a seal to be broken open;
the seal which Freud called repression.
Not a gradual process,
but a sudden breakthrough.
A reversal of meaning;
the symbolism suddenly understood.

        Norman O. Brown

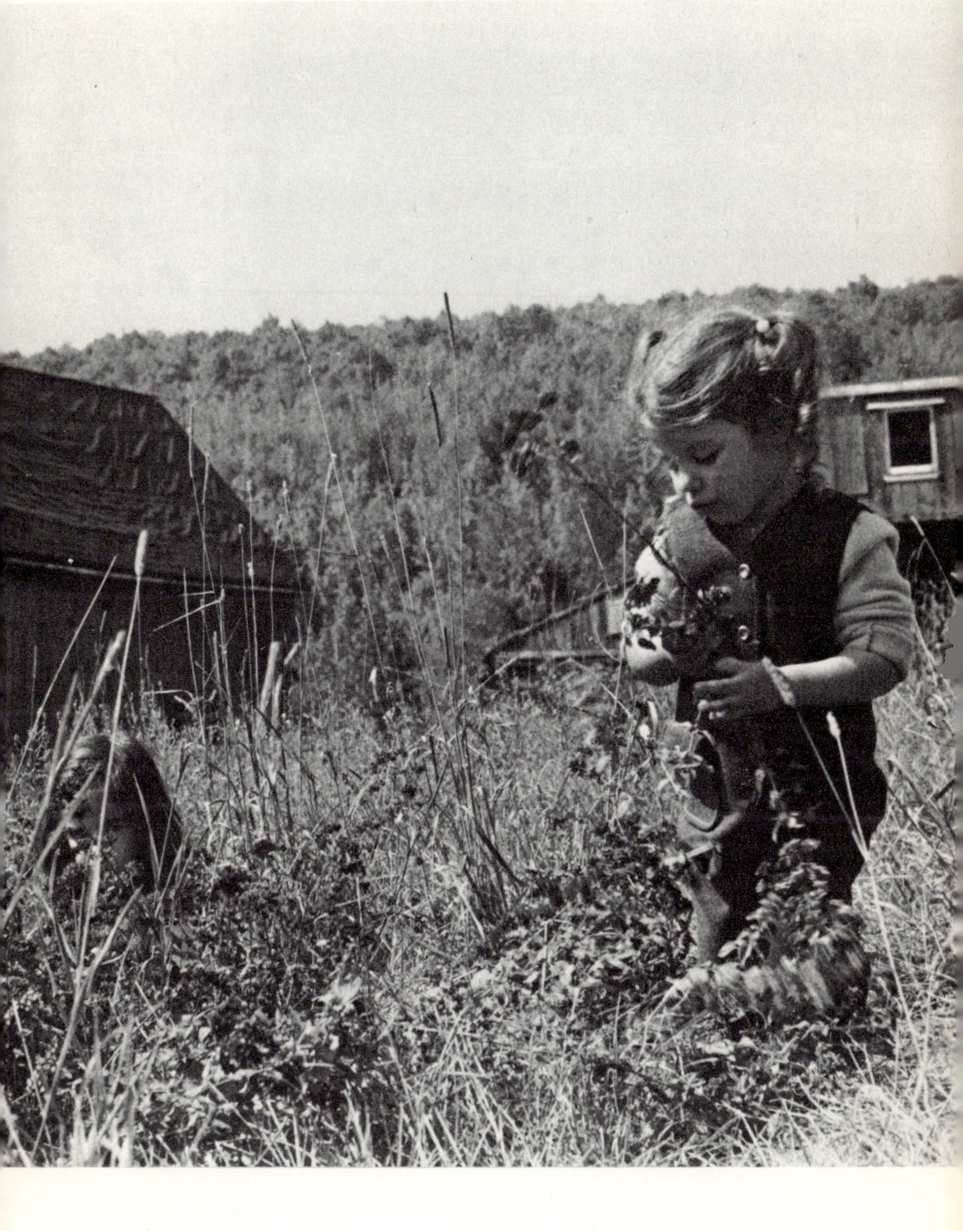

We are living through the closing chapters
of the established and traditional way of life.
We are in the early beginnings of a struggle,
which will probably last for generations,
to remake our civilization.
It is not a good time for politicians.
It is a time for prophets and leaders
and explorers and inventors and pioneers,
and for those who are willing to plant trees
for their children to sit under.

                     Walter Lippmann

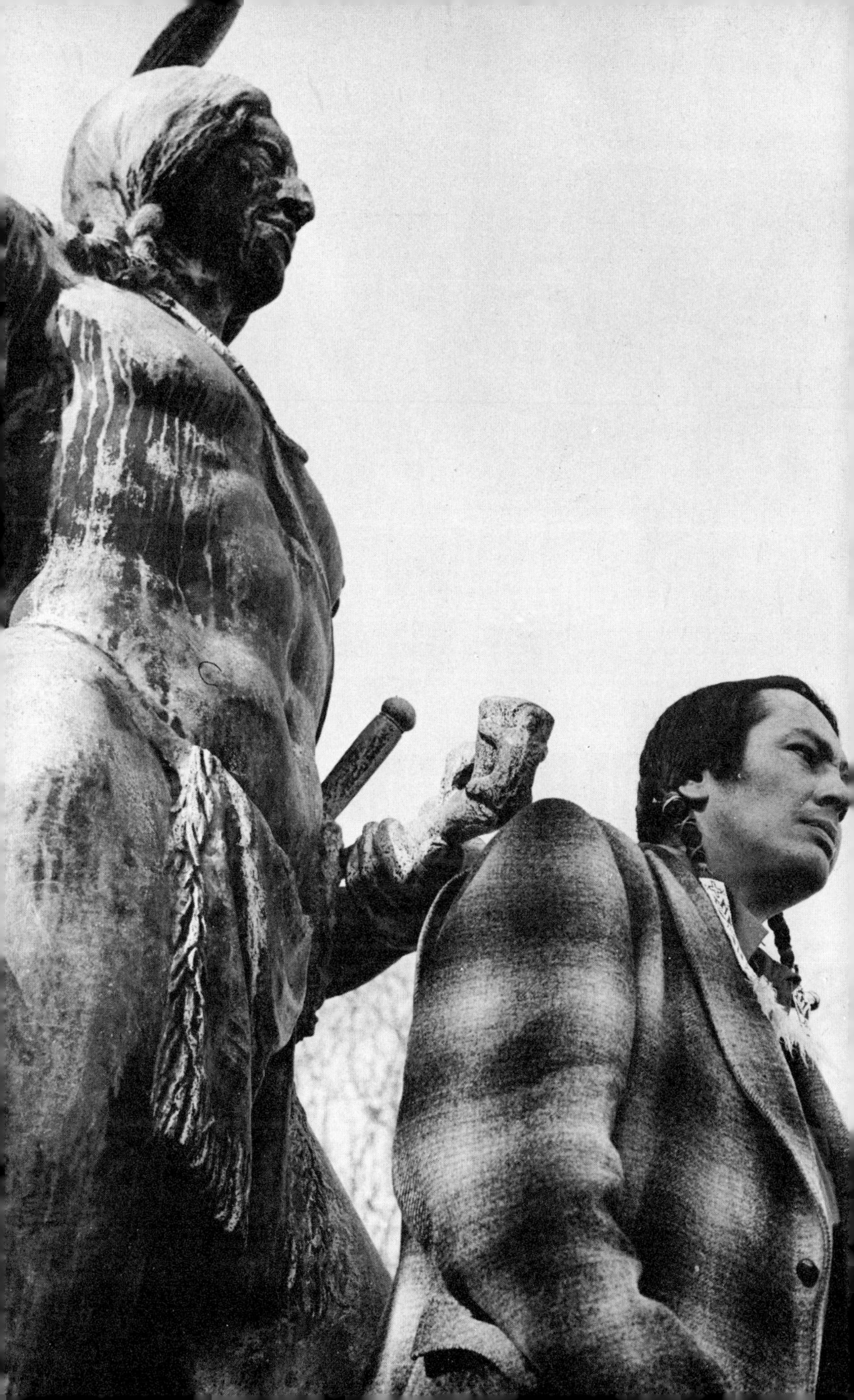

OTHERS AND ALL OTHERS

The natural high experience has among its sources nature and the self. It can also spring from relating to others. Just as you experience yourself as part of the world around you, you can also feel at one with the people around you. The more you discover of the fascinating uniqueness of each person you meet, the more you can respect your own. This is the self-enriching experience of brotherhood.

Reporter: At the Carnegie Hall concert, when everyone started storming the stage, were they talking to you as a person?

Melanie: Yeah, it was really a human thing. I felt that it was a very human contact. It was a very protective attitude from the audience. They were protective of me. I don't know why, but they were really kind. They weren't coming to ask me for anything.

After I had sung my songs and everybody got up on stage, there was one girl who was crying. I don't know why. After I was getting up to leave she started crying. It's almost embarrassing to tell but she was crying "Melanie, please don't go." It was really frightening.

I started crying when I left.

Interview with
Melanie Safka

The inner trip must be dealt with
in terms of our own past
not the past of an alien civilization.
Failure to heed this warning
is producing aberration upon aberration—
cultural mutations responding
to the stress of our crisis—
that just will not produce
the breakthrough in awareness
that we need.
     Ira Einhorn

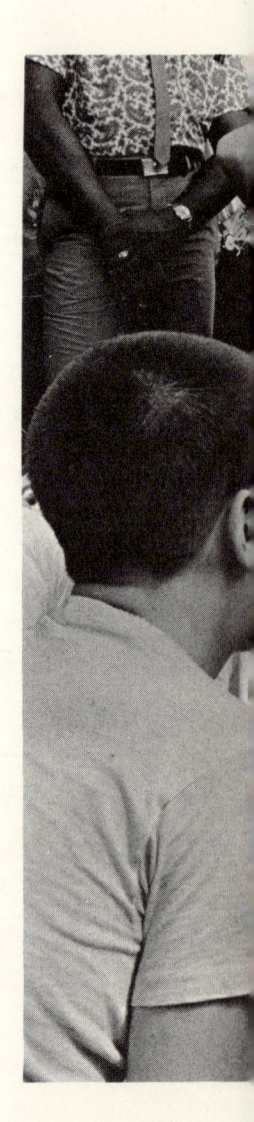

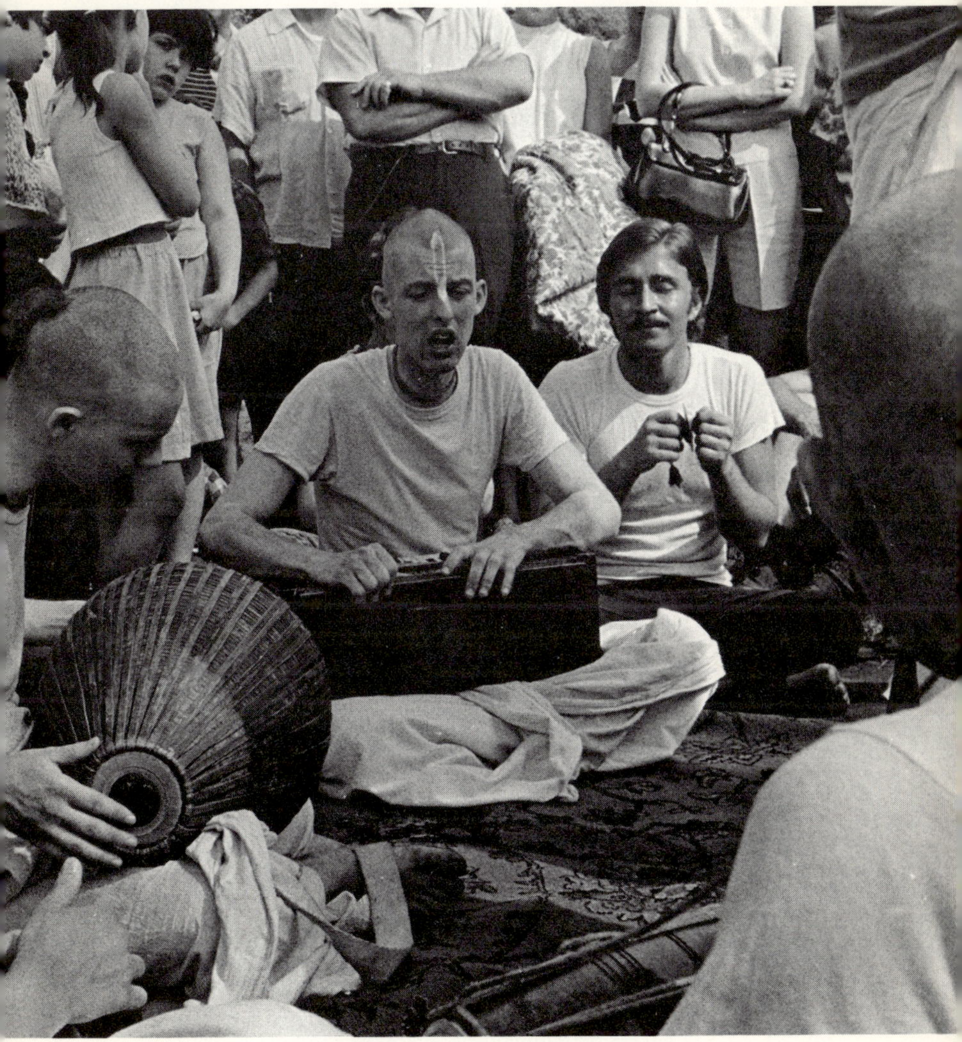

The act of giving—whether it's a smile
or something more tangible—
is almost always an "up."
The simplest and most obvious effect
is to make you feel good about yourself.
And as a result,
your clothes seem more comfortable,
your body works more smoothly,
everything is together...
You're on a high.
And one from which there is no crash
because it is naturally induced.

      Laurie Muir

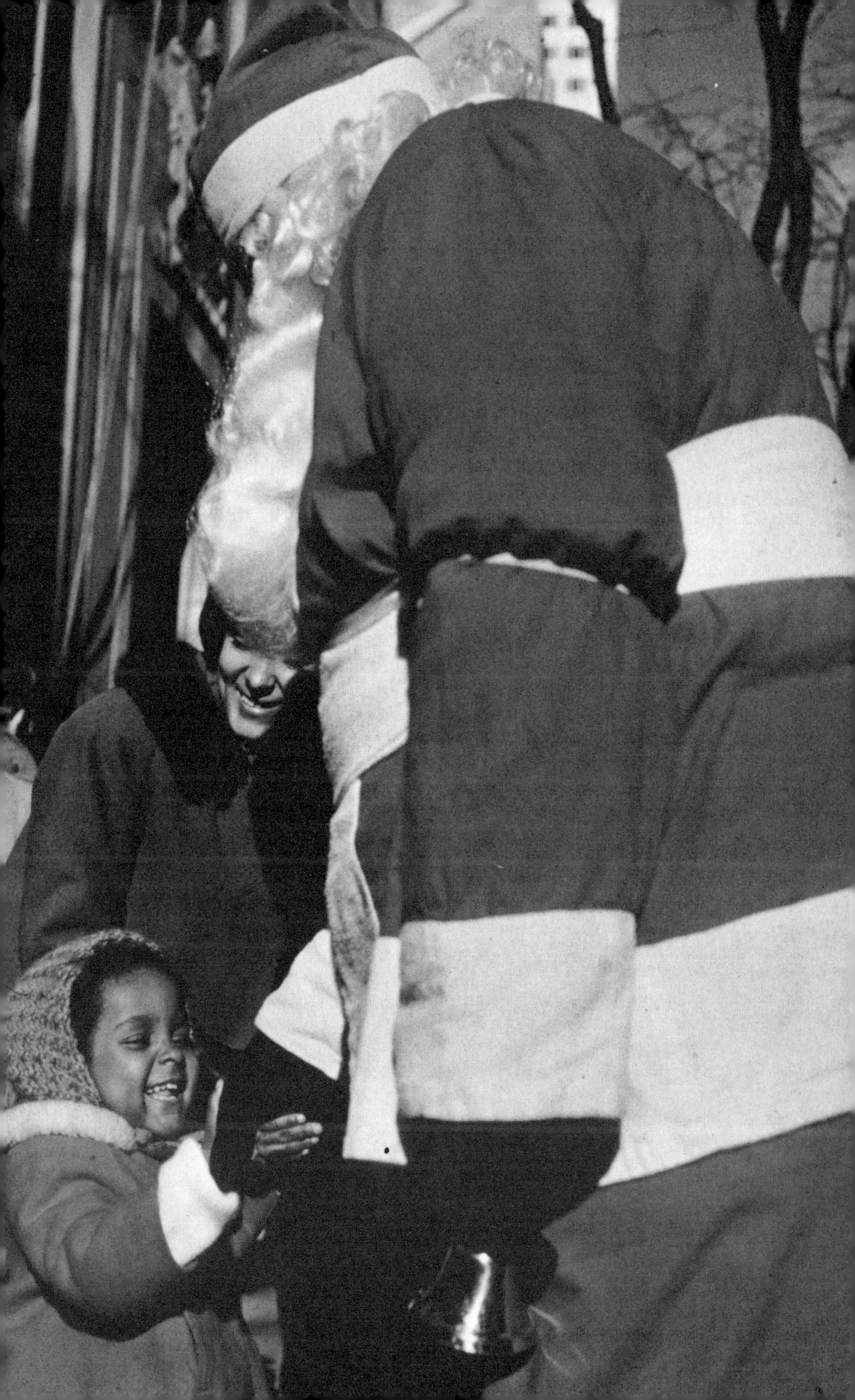

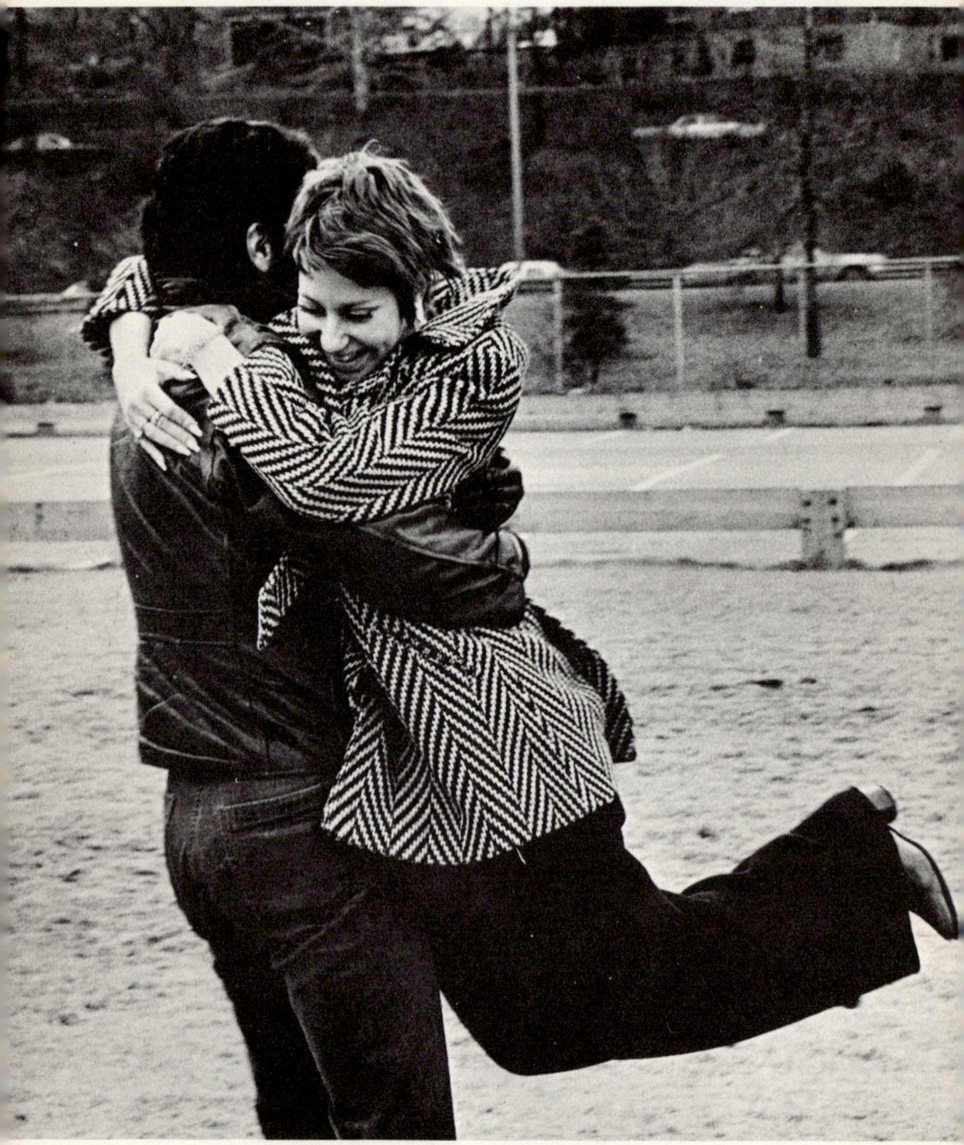

FACING LOVE

Only those who allow themselves to enter fully into all human experience can fully experience what love means. In love you are challenged to enter as deeply as possible into another person, a Thou, who faces you. In discovering what it is that unites the two of you in love, you begin to grasp the root of all things that live.

>Hardly anyone dares
>to face with open eyes
>the great delight of love.
>
>André Breton

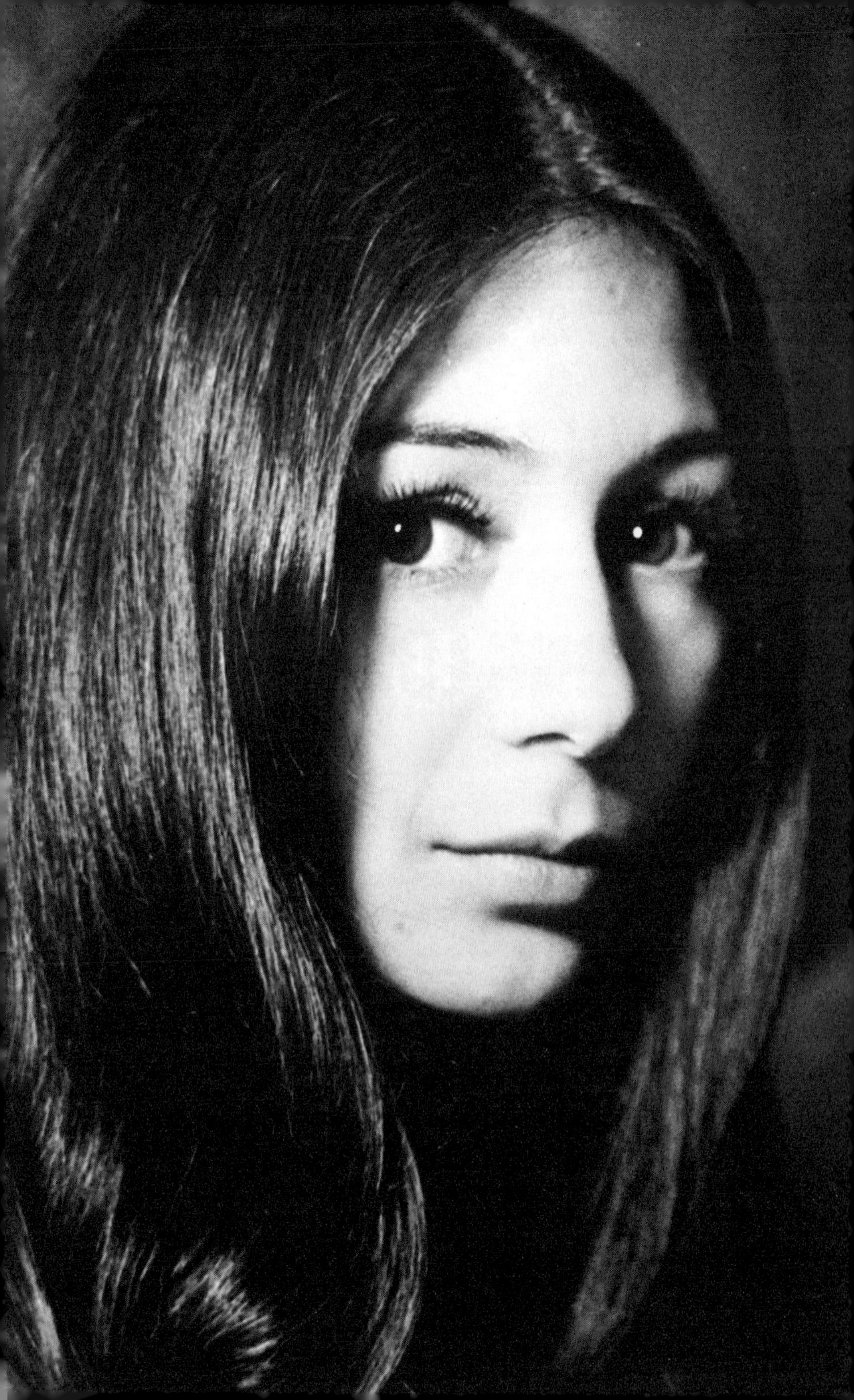

Yale looked at her in wonder, struck by the clear, clean beauty of her features. She had large, brown eyes that seemed to contain within them the wisdom of her race. Her face descended from high cheekbones to a firm chin. Her slightly angular jaw was a favorite of many artists depicting feminine beauty. He suddenly realized that Cynthia's features resembled his own imaginings of Ruth and Naomi in the Old Testament. In the years to come, as he knew Cynthia better, the thought would often recur to him that even beyond her own awareness she seemed to carry with her a racial warmth and understanding. Later, he would ask her many times if she realized that she had this transcendent beauty, and she would look at him and laugh, and tell him that perhaps it wasn't she at all, but something he had conjured in his own eyes and in his own brain.

Robert H. Rimmer

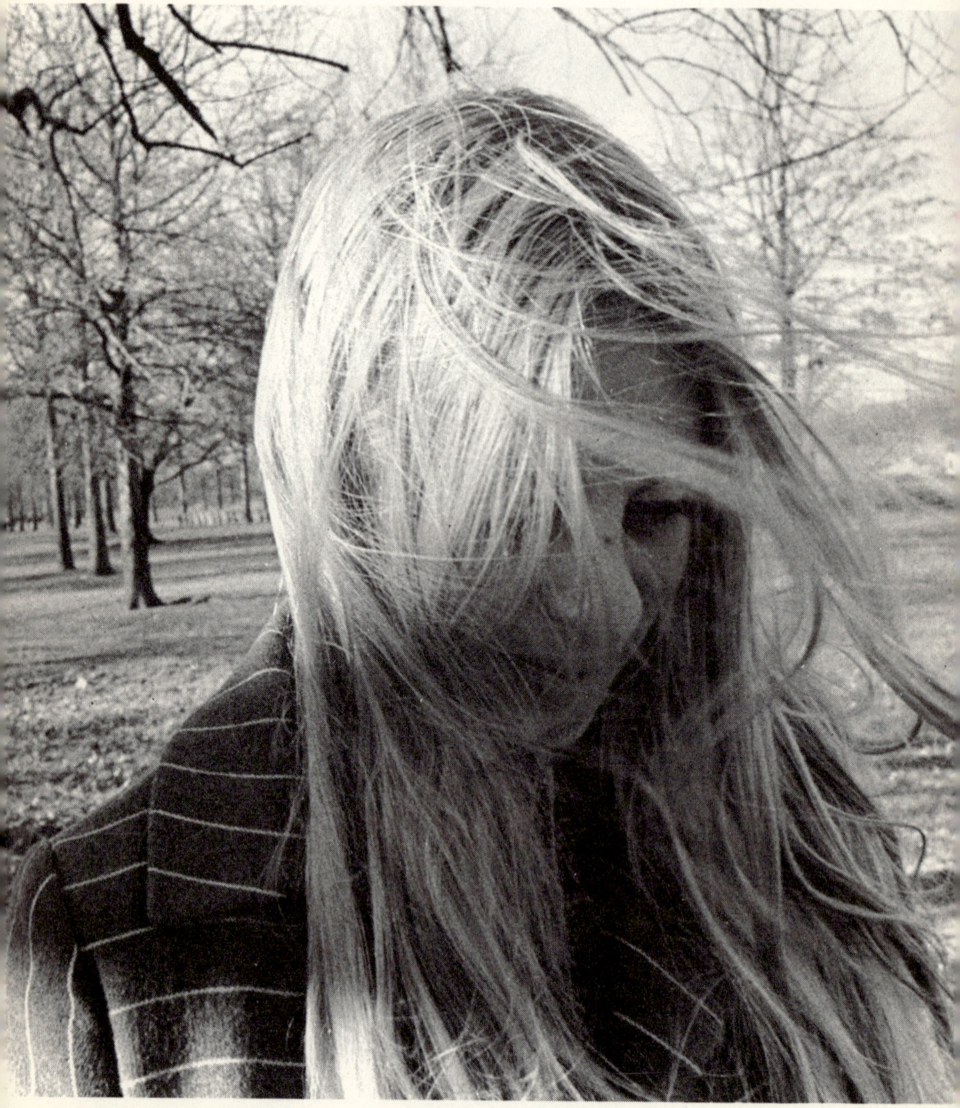

And yet, and yet,—
Seeing the tired city, and the trees so still
    and wet,—
It seemed as if all evenings were the same;
As if all evenings came,
Despite her smile at thinking of a kiss
With just such tragic peacefulness as this;
With just such hint of loneliness or pain;
The perfect quiet that comes after rain.

                  Conrad Aiken

TOGETHER FROM ETERNITY

The love relationship, when known most deeply, is not merely an affectionate and passionate experience. The experience is at once so ecstatic, so deep and integral that it seems to uncover a personal bond between lovers made ages ago in history. True love unveils a centuries-old bond of unity, a reality far more ancient than the short lives of the two in love. Here we are close to mystery.

>Before I knew you—
>look, the words are meaningless.
>You know very well that,
>when I saw you for the first time,
>I recognized you at once.
>
>André Breton

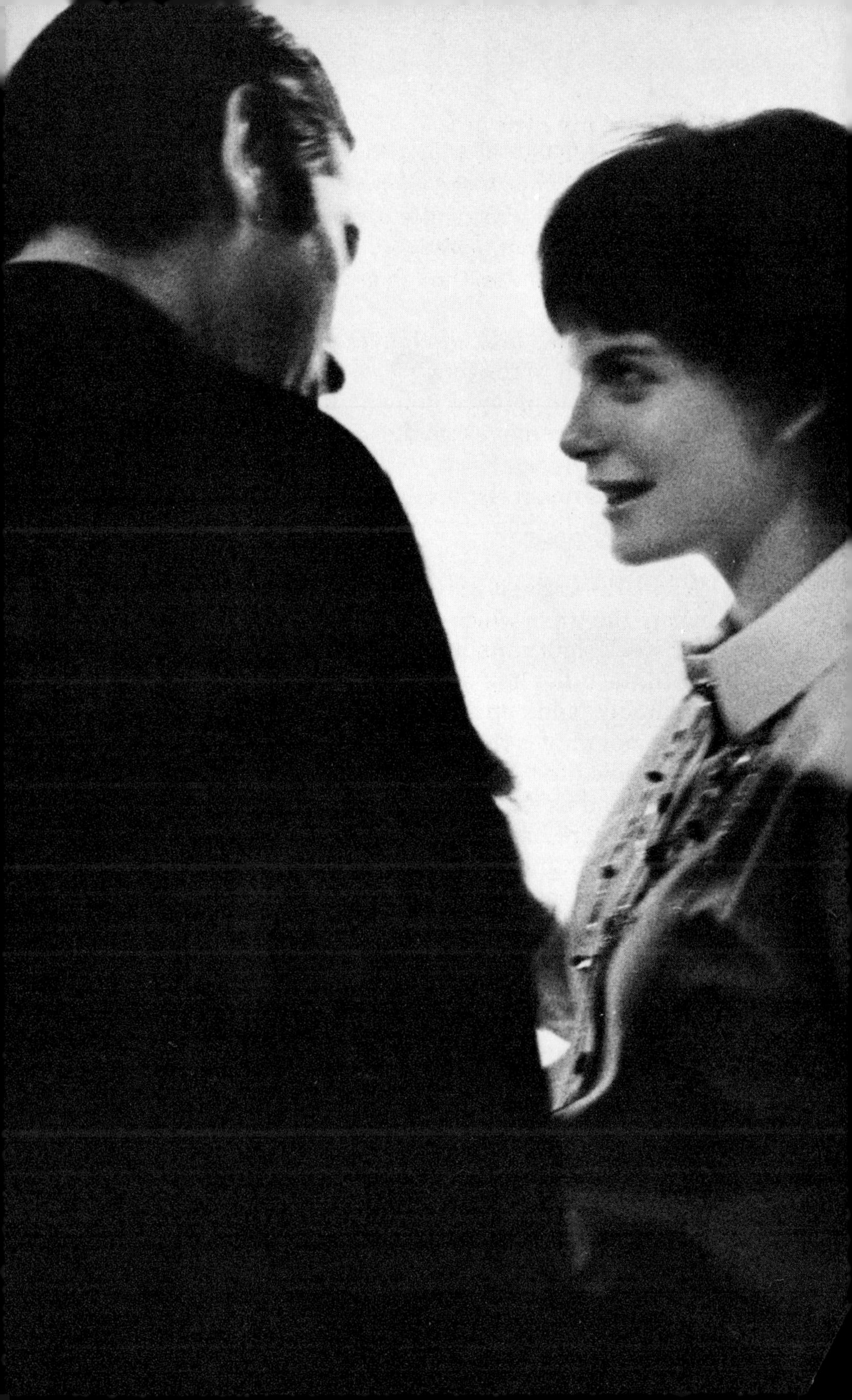

I believe, my little girl,
when people love as I love you,
they have always loved each other.
How would they recognize each other
if the soul had not always
contained an image, though a veiled one?

We are divided into two halves
the one open to the day,
and the other plunged in night, unconscious.
They live and move together
and communicate:
sometimes one feels this exchange
without really knowing it.

Where the springing stream goes to,
where the wave which submerges us comes from,
our weak sight cannot see.
Until the other half also
gradually lights up and is revealed.
Then not only is the fullness
of a whole life laid before us,
but behind us we find
that the dark barrier,
which hid from us half our being,
has been raised.

And we see how what seemed distinct and
    complete
with its own separate ways
was already unconsciously
in communication with the rest.

I greet you, my life,
with all that I am, was and can be.

           Thorbecke's Letters

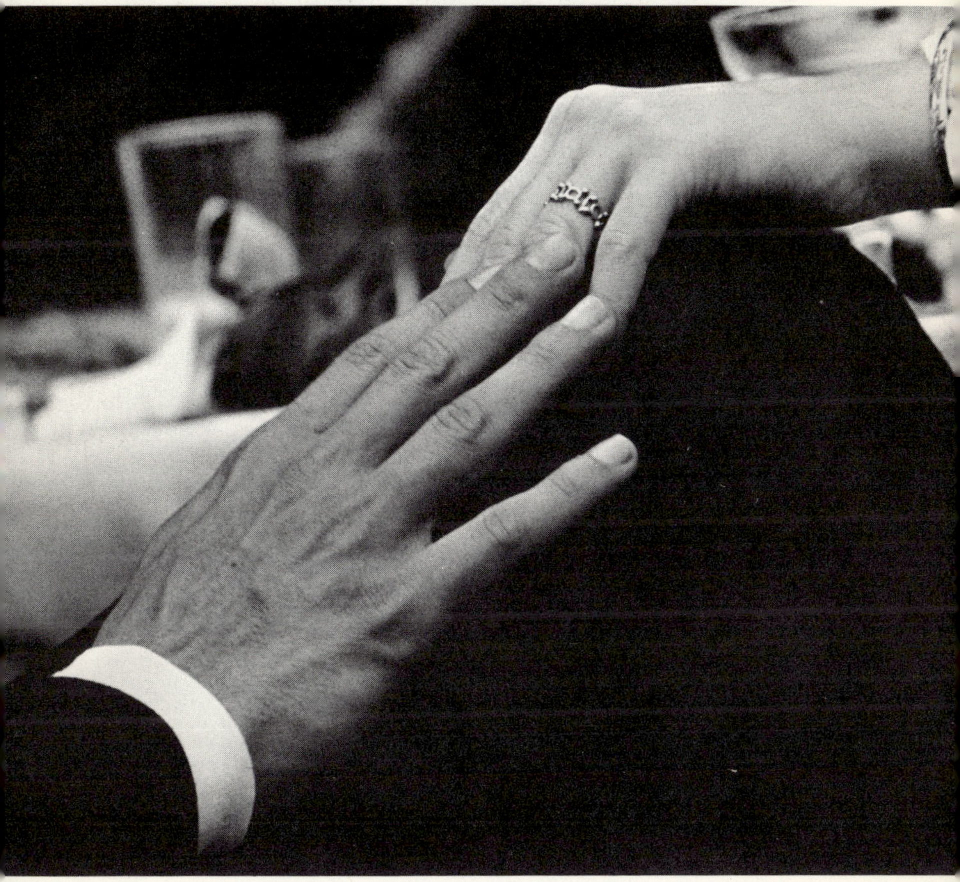

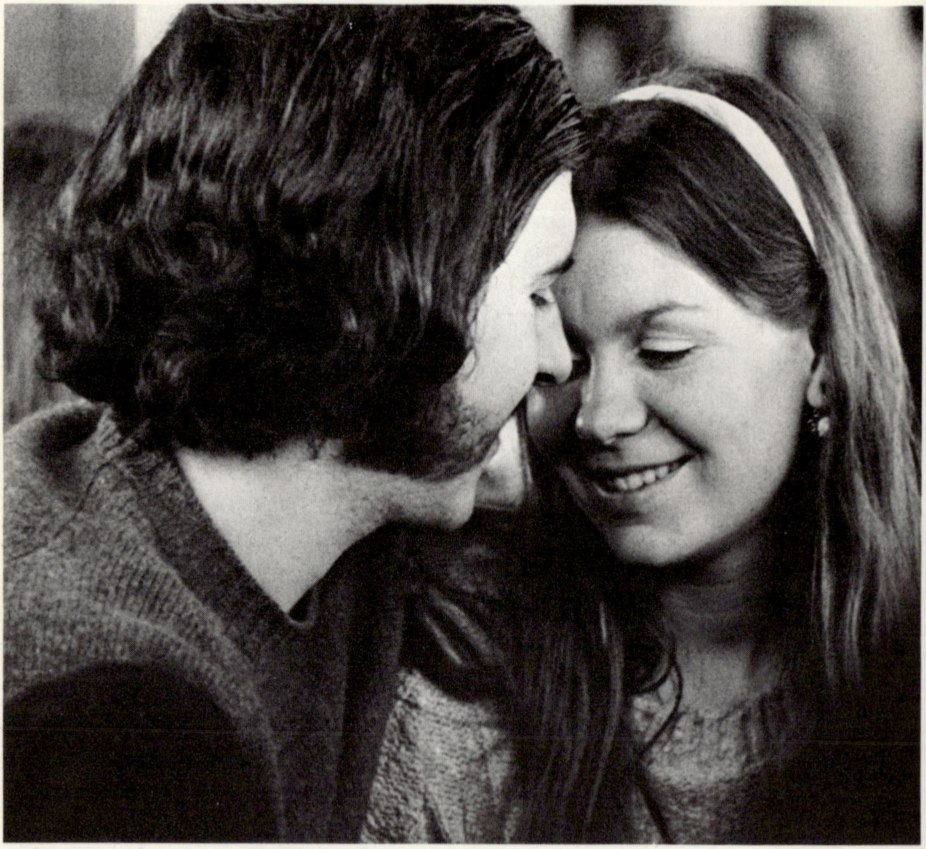

In the beginning, in truth,
nothing of all this existed.
From non-being there issues being.
This being changes into a Self.
The self existed first in the form
of the cosmic Person.
He looked and saw only himself.
He said: I *am*...
He desired another.
He became as large
as a man and woman embracing.
He divided into two.
So there was a husband and a wife.
This is why each man
is only a half.
The empty space is filled
by the woman.
He coupled with her.
So it is that men were created.

    Brihadâranyaka Upanishad

LOVE UNIFYING THE BOUNDLESS

If love cannot reach a thing, that thing does not exist. To those who experience the "soundless throbbing" of love, their human relationships are boundless and sources of limitless power. They know as their very own the enterprise of the universe and are united with its ultimate purpose. This is the high at its highest.

"Where have I come from, where did you pick me up?" the baby asked its mother.

She answered, half-crying, half-laughing, and clasping the baby to her breast: "You were hidden in my heart as its desire, my darling.

"You were in the dolls of my childhood's games; and when with clay I made the image of my god every morning, I made and unmade you then.

"You were enshrined with our household deity; in his worship I worshipped you.

"In all my hopes and my loves, in my life, in the life of my mother, you have lived.

"In the lap of the deathless Spirit who rules our home you have been nursed for ages."

Rabindranath Tagore

From this ocean of life,
in which we are immersed,
we are continually drawing something,
and we feel that our being,
or at least the intellect that guides it,
has been formed therein
by a kind of local concentration.
Philosophy can only be an effort
to dissolve again into the Whole...
But the enterprise
cannot be achieved in one stroke;
it is necessarily collective
and progressive.
It consists in an interchange
of impressions which,
correcting and adding to each other,
will end by expanding
the humanity in us
and making us even transcend it.

                Henri Bergson

Love is the river of life in this world.
Think not that ye know it
who stand at the little tinkling rill,
the first small fountain.

Not until you have gone through
the rocky gorges, and not lost the stream;
not until you have gone through
the meadow, and the stream has widened
and deepened until fleets
could ride on its bosom;
not until beyond the meadow
you have come
to the unfathomable ocean,
and poured your treasures
into its depths—
not until then
can you know what love is.

              Henry Ward Beecher